*M*ILESTONES

MILESTONES

A Catholic priest shows that
one of God's greatest gifts is a
sense of humour

THE LIGHT-HEARTED MEMOIRS OF
MONSIGNOR FREDERICK A. MILES, Prot. Ap.

McCrimmons
Great Wakering, Essex, England

The author would like to express his deep gratitude to
Matthew Pritchett (multi-award winning cartoonist)
for his front cover cartoon, and also to the Telegraph Media
Group for their kind permission in allowing the use of
Matt's prodigious talent.

Thanks also to Fran Godfrey for her encouragement
and for typing the manuscript.

First published in 2007 in the United Kingdom by
MCCRIMMON PUBLISHING CO. LTD.
10-12 High Street, Great Wakering, Essex SS3 0EQ
info@mccrimmons.com
www.mccrimmons.com

ISBN 978-0-855976-88-0

Cover illustration by Matt
Cover design and page layout by Nick Snode
Typeset in 11.5/13pt Bembo
Text pages printed on 100gsm Pavarotti Silk / Cover printed on 260gsm
Printed and bound by Thanet Press Ltd, Margate Kent, UK   E/0G

Contents

Foreword

The memoirs which follow this preamble are the collected experiences of a Catholic priest. But they are not necessarily what you might expect them to be. They are not 'holy' or theological reminiscences, but I would hate you to think that Monsignor Miles is not a holy or theologically-minded person. As this book goes into publication, I have known Mgr Miles for about ten years – and how I wish it were longer, because then I could have become a better person sooner.

I met Mgr Miles when he was Rector of St James's Church in the centre of London. I am a 'cradle Catholic' and my faith used not to be all that important to me. I attended Mass on Sunday mornings and on feast days – and that was about it. Then I heard a sermon preached by Mgr Miles on the subject of choice and free will. And, although I didn't realise it at the time, my life changed from that moment. All these years later, I can say that my faith is now the single most important thing in my life – and that change has been brought about through contact with Mgr Miles – and, of course, the intervention of the Holy Spirit. And I am only one of many who have been thus affected.

It is hard to avoid this foreword becoming an effusive paean to Frederick Miles, but I want you to understand what a remarkable man he is. He is a man of great faith and devoutness; his strict principles are never compromised; I have never seen him lose his temper or grow short of patience; his humility stems from honest self-knowledge and acceptance that all gifts come from God. In the years I have known him, I have discovered only one slight flaw – he is almost completely devoid of any sense of urgency! Although he is rarely late, he usually only arrives on time by the skin of his teeth. A couple of the stories he tells later will illustrate this small shortcoming! Mgr Miles is also completely incapable of telling a lie – regardless of the situation. I remember visiting him once, shortly after having had my hair re-styled. Vainly, I asked his opinion. "Well, Fran," he said, "It's not an improvement." Just one small example of his extraordinary honesty, and – because it was so funny – I wasn't in the slightest offended. Which leads me on to one of his most endearing qualities – and that is his great sense of humour and, more than that, his enormous sense of fun. He loves the eccentricities of mankind and is quick to see the humour in just about any situation. Like so many people he has pains and physical debilities, yet he bears his burdens bravely, and often humorously.

All of the above might give you some idea of what to expect in these memoirs. It's been my privilege and pleasure to type his anecdotes as he dictated them. Be prepared to smile and to laugh out loud. But remember also that this is only one part of an extraordinary man who is loved and respected by all who know him.

FRAN GODFREY

CHAPTER I

The 'Miserable' Years

I was a miserable child. I don't suppose I can blame anyone else for this conviction: it's just the way I remember it. There are very few things I do remember about my childhood but I have a recollection of burying my head in a towel in the kitchen when I was talking with my mother at the age of about eleven. I can't recall the precise reason why; I have a feeling it was because I had lost a rather important bit of a toy glider I had been given. It was a metal fixture in the nose of the glider and when this bit came adrift the glider lost its balance and never flew properly again. I don't think that did any more than colour my recollections of childhood. Nor do I think it was an abiding source of sadness.

This was an early memory, but not the earliest. My first memory was of a minor incident which occurred when I was about two years old. My mother was visiting her family in Cork. There were her parents and two of her sisters living in Blarney Street in Cork City. The only recollection I really have of this visit is of a tobacco tin belonging to my grandfather. It was dark metal, round in shape and with a knob on top for removing the lid. It was given to me to absorb my attention as I sat under the table. I yearned to possess this tobacco tin, but, of course, did not dare say anything about it. The tobacco tin belonged to my grandfather – and that was that. That is about the only recollection I have of visiting Ireland in 1927. In 1947 I was to visit Ireland once again. By this time the war was over and travel to Ireland could be resumed; so I went with my mother. We stayed, once again, in Blarney Street with my Aunt Lou (my mother's sister, Louise) and Aunt Nan – another sister.

As to being a miserable child, I can't honestly say that I had any real reasons for being so. I was born in 1925, the fifth child of six, to Patrick Joseph and Elizabeth Josephine Miles. My father was from County Mayo and my mother from County Cork. They had met when my father, a member of the Royal Irish Constabulary, was Head Constable in Dublin Castle. My mother was a nurse in a psychiatric hospital in the same city. They married and set up home in Halliday Square, Dublin, where two of my three brothers were born. In 1922 the Royal Irish Constabulary was disbanded when the Republic of Ireland was set up, and members of that body were invited by the British Government to immigrate to England and take up posts in the Metropolitan Police. I think many members of the RIC had the impression that, because they had joined a force set up by the British Government to control the activities of the IRA, they were to some extent despised by their own community. My father did, in fact, immigrate to England, but he did not choose to take up the offer of a position in the Metropolitan Police. Instead he bought, with his gratuity, a property in Dunmow in Essex. It was called Bridge House and we lived there until about 1927. As I was only two when we left, I have no memories of this home at all.

It was in 1923 that my elder sister was born, and I followed in 1925. The reason my father decided to settle in Dunmow was, I think, because the Hewitt family had bought property there. The Hewitts were Irish Protestants: Fred Hewitt had been in the RIC and our families knew each other well even before we left Dublin. I have some notion that my father thought he could make a living by being a market gardener; but this idea, I believe, was soon given up and he took a job as a clerk in the factory of Crittall's Metal Windows. He used to cycle each day from Dunmow to his place of work in Braintree – nine miles away. After a couple of years a move was made to the Braintree area. We lived in a house which I do not remember in Bocking Church Street – Bocking being a suburb of Braintree. After a time in Bocking Church Street we moved into a council house in Wordsworth Road where we stayed until 1935.

Our next move was prompted by the imminent arrival of my younger sister, Patricia. I think that it was then that I ceased to be miserable. This was in part due to my happiness at having a baby sister, and in part due to the fact that my elder sister, Rene, (who was by then 11) was more taken up with mothering Pat than persecuting me! It might seem unfair to accuse Rene of persecuting me because, in all honesty, I can remember no particular incidents. I just have a vague recollection of her ganging up with my brother Gerry to make my life miserable. But I would hate either of them to carry the guilt of this to their graves! I did, after all, cheer up.

CHAPTER II

The Early Schooling Years

I began my schooling at the age of five by attending the convent school in Bocking. Saint Francis School was a tiny establishment run by Franciscan nuns. Close to the school was an orphanage run by the same nuns. The girls from there, dressed in thick serge tunics with pale blue figured pinafores, stood out from the rest of us. I remember among the orphans, there was a dwarf-like figure whose name was Lina. She was Portuguese, spoke little English and was very introspective. I used to feel sometimes that the nuns were a bit hard on Lina, who we all believed had had a very hard childhood – little short of persecution. I remember seeing Lina have a caning in public (all the caning was in public) when she was being particularly stubborn. Having said this, I have to add that the canings were rare. Not as rare as they are today, of course, but the instilling of discipline was done differently then and I think I would be disappointing many if I did not trot out the cliché "It never did me any harm!" It was an extraordinary little school – the only place for Catholic children to be educated in that area. There were two separate classrooms, until eventually a third was formed by partitioning the larger into two smaller rooms. In the Infant Class we were taught to read and write using slates with slate pencils – not the graphite we use today. Our arithmetic lessons featured the use of the abacus, and all these proceedings were supervised by an irascible lady who had a peculiar little brown hat. Her name was Miss Dalton.

The next class up was a smaller area of the main classroom. We had nice desks in the top class with inkwells. Every so often we took some time out to mix powder with water and produce the ink with which we wrote in a kind of grey spidery writing with steel dip-pens – quite an advance from the slate. Fountain pens were not allowed. It goes without saying that Laszlo Biro had not yet done his stuff!

The main classroom was dominated by a large partially-glass ceiling. This room was said to have been the studio of one Madame Arendrup. She was an imposing lady not by reason of her stature but rather by the aristocratic glint in her eye. She was a member of the Courtauld family, therefore very rich. I believe it was she who donated funds for the building of the Convent where the Franciscans sisters lived. Madame Arendrup was an artist who liked to paint pictures of animals. There was a large ring attached to one wall of our schoolroom. To this, we were told, Mme Arendrup would tether the animal of the day, so to speak – the odd cow or sheep perhaps.

Also in the main classroom there was a high desk at which the headmistress of the school occasionally sat. Her name was Sister Mary Elizabeth. She was Scottish, a bit fussy and prepared all of us in due course for our First Confession and First Holy Communion. For these little instructions we would gather around her high desk and she would descend from the heights to talk to us. The other desk was occupied by a powerful nun, Mother Mary Michael. She sat at a table and by dint of her forthright personality and penetrating voice dominated the whole room. If she thought you were promising in your last year or so in the school she would make you sit around this desk doing what, for most of us seemed to be higher mathematics, though it was still far removed from Calculus or slide rules. In a very non-politically correct way, it was only the boys – and none of the girls – who were invited to sit around her table.

The rear part of the schoolroom was eventually partitioned so that the unfortunate teacher in that section – who had previously been obliged to do her teaching in opposition to the noise coming from the main teaching area – might have some privacy. It was in this room that I was occasionally called to the desk of the nun who taught there, and in my day that was Sr Mary Cuthbert. I do not think that she had ever been to a university, but she had attended a school in Durham where she had completed her School Certificate and Higher Certificate, no doubt with great distinction. She was lively and good-humoured and was doted upon by the otherwise fierce Mother Mary Michael.

When I made my First Holy Communion at the age of seven, Sr Mary Elizabeth presented me with a shiny white prayer book with gilt edges. It was while I was reading this book – one day – doing my best to read it I suppose would be more honest – that I met the word 'neighbour'. I looked at the word for some time and then said 'neighbour'! The realisation hit me suddenly that I could read. I suppose the fact that I was reading this little prayer book at the age of seven instead of the 'Hotspur' or some other boys' comic could be seen as something of a pointer to my decision to train for the priesthood.

It is hard to say when I was first aware that I wanted to become a priest. In my very young years I went through the usual phase of wanting to be a train driver/'bus driver/pilot, but I had abandoned such ideas by the age of nine. I do know that when Sister Mary Cuthbert learned that I wished to study for the priesthood she set about teaching me Latin, while the other children spent the time writing compositions. Largely because of Sr Mary Cuthbert's teaching I spent only a few weeks in the first form at St Edmund's before being moved up a year. The result was that I was ordained a year earlier than I would otherwise have been. It is true that I had been a daily Mass server at the Convent chapel – the only place where Catholics in Braintree could hear Mass. We had no church. But about the year 1936 Father Walter P Walsh was appointed to Braintree and immediately set about plans for building a church. There was very little money in the parish, but a friend and I used to cycle round, visiting certain parishioners on Saturday mornings on what was called an "outdoor collection". Fr Walsh had asked us to undertake this work with a view to collecting money for a site and the building of a church. He had been appointed to Braintree where, as well there being no church, there was no presbytery – just the Convent chapel at Bocking, where a room was provided for him. He was a very zealous priest of about 35 years of age. It may have been his zeal which impressed a member of the Courtauld family – Richard Courtauld – and resulted in his buying a site and providing a church. It was situated in a very central part of Braintree and eventually a presbytery was built beside the church. The church was opened on 31st August, 1939 and dedicated, paradoxically, to Our Lady, Queen of Peace: three days later we were at war with Germany.

Fr Walsh was very serious-minded, and it came as quite a surprise to me to discover that he had a passion for cricket. I do not think he ever played the game at any level; but I do know that he suggested to me one day in 1948 that we should go to Lords and see, not one of the stars of the day, Don Bradman, but Keith Miller – a dashing bowler and batsman in that 1948 touring side known as the Invincibles. I accepted with alacrity, and he drove us up to London in his little Austin Seven. We had a great day in the sun at Lords; we saw neither Miller nor Bradman batting, but we did enjoy the spectacle of Keith Miller's magnificent fast bowling. Many years later I was to meet Keith Miller and got to know him over a long period. Indeed I attended his wedding late in life to Marie. They got married in the village church at Stoke Poges. Keith had been stationed near there while he was serving in the Royal Australian Air Force towards the end of the war.

But I have digressed. To return to Fr Walsh, I suppose he had as much influence upon my decision to enter the seminary as any other single priest who had been in charge of the parish at

Braintree. In the first instance he applied to the Bishop of Brentwood to adopt me as a student for the priesthood. I was then aged 12 years. As there was no positive response from the bishop, Fr Walsh wrote to Cardinal Arthur Hinsley to accept me for the Diocese of Westminster. One day in the summer of 1938 my eldest brother, Kevin, took me to Archbishop's House in Westminster where I had an interview with Cardinal Hinsley and the seminary Rector, Mgr Francis Bickford, who was the President of St Edmund's College in Ware. I was very happy to feel that everything was now set for my entry to the seminary.

CHAPTER III

The Acquisitive Years

On a less serious note I have to confess at this point to being a confirmed 'swapper'.

I hardly ever had any money – as my family was far from wealthy – so the only way of acquisition was by swapping. It began really when I was about six or seven years old. It was my practice, walking to and from school, to scrutinise the gutters and pavement. There one would, on occasion, find a discarded Players cigarettes packet with – if I was lucky – a card inside it. I collected cards depicting motor cars, cricketers and animals – I remember there was a whole series featuring chickens; but I was more interested in the sportsmen. Thus I acquired a currency for swapping.

Some years later I inherited a stamp collection – quite a good collection, in fact, from one of my brothers – but when I found a friend at school who was a budding philatelist, I persuaded him to part with his pair of roller skates in exchange for my stamp album. Thus began my swapping career proper. I enjoyed the skates for a time, but eventually a small piano-accordion found its way onto the swapping market and the skates had to go. There now opened a new phase in my life – I can't say that it was the start of a stunning musical career; but it was the beginning of a succession of musical instruments at which I tried my hand. After the piano-accordion came the flute and, in rapid succession, the clarinet, the bugle and finally the mouth-organ – which I am proud to say I have to this day. I also have memories of trying to produce a tune from a Jew's Harp, sometimes called a jaws' harp. This little harp did not engage my attention for very long because it was not a great instrument for producing a melody – at least not in my hands – or jaw! However, the mouth-organ was a very superior instrument. This particular one was called a harmonica; it had a valve at the side that you could press to provide semi-tones. (I am still open to swaps if you like the sound of this.) At nearly every school concert – at this stage I was about fourteen years of age – I was given top-billing; well actually, I was given a ten-minute slot in which I played a medley of modern tunes – the greatest hits of Carmen Miranda and the like. I had them dancing in the aisles! When I consider it today, I don't know how I ever had the nerve to stand up in front of an audience (of sorts) and attempt to entertain them! Perhaps I should rootle the instrument out one of these days and resume my musical career!

I cannot really remember when money first changed hands for any of my possessions. When the youth club closed down in Braintree (we lost the premises), I asked the parish priest if I might have the boxing gloves that had been used there – regularly by me. They were evil-smelling, really ghastly; they smelt like the Wrath of God, you might say, except that God was not the culprit; the fault lay firmly with a malodorous fellow who was something of a stranger to the bath-tub. I suppose I should really have kept them hanging out of the window on a string, or a piece of hairy twine – as the Irish might say, because nobody else in the house could bear to be in the same room as these gloves. Speaking of 'hairy twine', the story goes that Tony O'Reilly, the Ireland rugger wing three-quarter in the 1950's, once walked into the England dressing room before a international match and called out, "Does anyone once have a bit of hairy twine for me boots?" Such enviable calm, such panache!

Anyway, back to the malodorous boxing gloves, I remember taking them with me to the Knights of St Columba holiday camp, near Maldon in Essex. I went from tent to tent offering these gloves to anybody who was prepared to have a bout with me. The only taker I can remember was a stringy fellow – much too genteel really to have anything to do with these evil gloves. Nevertheless he put them on and I squared up to him and suddenly received the most stinging left hook to my right ear that I had ever encountered. I boxed on – ears ringing – until such time as I could reasonably call a halt. The gloves were put away in my tent. They were never used again. My memory clouds over when I try to recall what happened to them; I can guess that they continued stinking until they *actually* rotted instead of just *smelling* as if they had. I never had the nerve to offer them for swap, and that was the end of my swapping career.

Out of respect for my dear younger sister, Patricia, I feel that there is one other confession I must make at this point. Pat had a very large doll; a life-sized baby doll, really. I was about twelve. The nuns at the Convent school asked to borrow the doll for a pivotal role in the Nativity Play. I cannot remember how the doll was brought to the school; but I vividly remember how it was returned to Pat. The nuns asked me to carry it home. They didn't even wrap it up. I walked the two miles home from school, during which time I was subjected to much abuse. Rough boys from other schools taunted me as I passed them while I was carrying this great doll. I was mortified. I offer this by way of mitigation for my later actions. It was about six months later that a friend and I suspended this doll from a beam in a store-room at the back of our house. He had an airgun and we pelted this thing with shots at almost point-blank range, until it was studded with pellets. It was unpardonable, but the only act of violence in my entire life. And Pat had gone off the doll anyway since I had named it The Brute. I would like to say that we buried the creature decently; but I cannot. This shooting incident in 1938 finally exorcised all the shame and abuse it had occasioned me on its journey with me through the streets.

CHAPTER IV

The Early Years at St Edmund's

It was about two weeks after the outbreak of war in September 1939 that Fr Walsh drove my mother and me across country to St Edmund's College, the place where I was to spend a total of 24 years of my life.

One of the first things to which I had to get accustomed, was the naming of the different classes. In most schools you get Form 1, Form 2 etc. At St Edmund's the differentiation of classes was done on the classical pattern. And so you would have – at the youngest level – Rudiments, then Grammar, Syntax, Poetry and Rhetoric. Rhetoric 1 and 2 were, therefore, the first and second sixth forms. I don't know of any other school which uses this system.

It was while I was in Poetry (the equivalent of the fifth form) that I discovered a great love of the work Geoffrey Chaucer in his *Canterbury Tales*. I used to listen to recordings made by Professor Neville Coghill – reading the text of Chaucer in the old language, as it was written and as he perceived it to be pronounced. In this way I learned enormous chunks of Chaucerian texts, many of which I can still quote to this day. Not a particularly useful accomplishment, but it amuses me! Today, if anyone still studies Chaucer at school, it is often in modern English.

I suppose what I enjoyed most about Chaucer was his remarkable eye for detail. For instance, when he came to describe a Canterbury pilgrim, the famous Miller, he does not just tell you that the miller was "a stout carl for the nonce", he adds that "upon the cop right of his nose he had a werte and thereon stood a tuft of haires, reed as the bristles of a sowes ear."

There are several words which I have adopted into my own vocabulary – one example being the word "gipoun". This is a garment worn by mediaeval soldiers immediately under a piece of chain-mail. When it rained, the gipoun became stained by rust. So, when Chaucer wanted to describe one of the pilgrims as having a soiled over-garment (a habergoun), he tells us "his habergoun was al bismotered as it were a gipoun." In my own life, my 'gipoun' is the name I have given to the garment worn by prelates. It's a sort of cape and its proper name is manteletta. I should add that my only reason for calling it a gipoun is because it's a lovely Chaucerian word, not because it's stained with rust!

To digress further, you can't really think of the magnificent English language without thinking of William Shakespeare. Most people have little idea of how many of the words we use regularly were coined by Shakespeare. Apparently he used almost eighteen thousand different words in his many writings – about ten percent of which he simply made up: words like, *critical, hurry, hint, gust, frugal, radiance* and so many more. Personally I have always had a fondness for *bubukles* and *whelks*, as displayed by the unfortunate Bardolph in Henry V. It appeared to be a severe Shakespearian version of acne; which leads me on to tell you about an advertisement I found in a nineteenth century liturgical reference book. Why it was in that particular book I cannot imagine, but the ad proudly proclaimed that the product was an effective remedy for acne, pimples and 'all manner of cutaneous visitations'. In those days, it seems, you could not simply have a spot, you had to be cutaneously visited!

Back to College. At the time of my joining, it was a gloomy place. The windows were reinforced by sandbags to protect the glass against exploding bombs. In fact, there never were any bombs; but one night two large mines were dropped – one of which exploded in a field on the far side of the A10 London to Cambridge Road, about 300 yards from the College. Despite this distance many windows on the front of the College were blown out – even the stained glass windows at the east end of the Chapel did not escape damage. Apart from that there were no other alarums until the V1 – the flying bomb, known to the phlegmatic English as the 'Doodlebug'. Doodlebugs were pilot-less aircraft loaded with explosives which flew noisily for a period of time until the fuel ran out. They then went silent and glided down to explode upon impact. Most of these bombs were directed at London; but to relieve the inhabitants of our capital city of constant bombardment, British fighter pilots would either shoot them down (a risky procedure because their explosive power was considerable) or, so we were told, would fly along beside the Doodlebug with the wing of the Spitfire or Hurricane ready to tip the Doodlebug out of the sky causing it to stall and fall to the ground where it would do the minimum damage to property and people.

I remember looking out of my window one morning when I was awoken by the heavy chug-chug of a V1. When the chugging ceased I stood at the window, waiting with some apprehension. In fact it glided for about a mile before it came down near the village of Collier's End.

When I was eighteen and eligible for military service I signed on for the Royal Navy. It was compulsory to register for military service and one could express a preference for which branch of the services one wished to serve in. In the event, I was never called up because Cardinal Bernard Griffin succeeded in securing exemption from military service for all students who had been accepted for the priesthood before 1939.

CHAPTER V

The OTC Years

Although exempt from military service, I didn't entirely escape from all involvement with matters military. Between the ages of 15 and 18 the boys in the school were given no choice: they were all conscripted into the OTC – the Officer Training Corps. Two afternoons a week we were paraded – occasionally in uniform, but quite often in mufti or, if there was a field exercise involving lying about under hedges and in fields, we would wear old clothes. After we had fallen in, we would be given instructions for the afternoon. Sometimes the exercises would involve one platoon taking up defensive positions and the others – the enemy – would advance upon that platoon. Sometimes we would work on the 'sand table'. This represented a section of terrain with hills, trees and hedgerows onto which there would be planned some military manoeuvre. At other times we would receive lectures in class: these would involve the structure and handling of the rifle, or aircraft recognition with the use of silhouettes of German and British planes, bombers and fighters.

Speaking of army instructions, I am reminded of a Sergeant-Major who, while instructing the platoon on the drill for fixing bayonets, told the lads, "When I says 'fix', you don't fix; but when I says 'bayonets' you whips 'em out, wops 'em on and lets 'em bide awhile." What an extraordinary instruction to still remember verbatim after 55 years!

Less enjoyable for me was the parade-ground work. We performed in Sections or Platoons. A Section consisted of seven soldiers and a Platoon of twenty-one men. All kinds of manoeuvres were carried out on the parade ground. Most of them were fairly straightforward – such as counter-marching, in which the whole Platoon would be marched to one end of the parade ground and turned about by means of a counter-march in the opposite direction. More complicated was the manoeuvre involving the formation of A Hollow Square. This would be when the Commanding Officer wished to explain something in detail, with his troops around him. It was tidier to have it like that; but it was no easy manoeuvre. The practice was to explain to the troops the word of command, and then tell them what their reaction should be. For example, "On the command, 'Quick March' the Platoon will advance in line, and then on the command, 'About turn', the Platoon will proceed in the opposite direction after facing about. The 'About Turn' command (it would be explained to the troops) would be given as the right foot came to the ground. After the command, one further pace would be taken with the left foot and then the soldier would turn himself about lifting up the feet with a one-two-three movement and then setting off in the reverse direction with the right foot. As you will have noticed, this was fairly complicated. It was always necessary to explain a manoeuvre in detail to the soldiers. Thus we would hear "On the command ..." and the instructions would follow. For example, "On the command, 'Fall out' – troops will come to attention, turn to the right, take one step forward and then disperse." More complicated moves, some of which no one had the foggiest idea how to execute, had to be explained in greater detail. The story is told of a Commanding Officer who asked a soldier who was giving words of command on the Parade Ground, "Do you know how to get the men to form a Hollow Square?" The soldier was confident, but didn't really know his own limitations – so he embarked upon the task of getting the men to form a Hollow Square. His technique was to explain: "On the command, 'Form an 'Oller Square', troops will – form an 'Oller Square'. There was a pause for dramatic effect and then he bellowed, 'Form an 'Oller Square!'. It really wasn't as simple as that; in fact, what he should have done was explain to the troops what precisely each rank did when the command was given. Utter chaos ensued. Nothing remotely resembling an 'Oller Square emerged from the disorder. It was back to the drawing board. To this day I could not form an 'Oller Square' – neither on my own nor in a platoon!

I have already mentioned the idiosyncrasies of army commands. We were taught the vital requirements of a good marksman. I did think that a steady arm and a good eye would feature among the essentials for accurate shooting. But apparently not: the army dictum was: "physical fitness, determination and nerve-control." Woe betides anyone who tried to introduce such notions as a steady arm and a sharp eye – these did not figure in the Army-approved list. I apparently was sufficiently possessed of 'physical fitness, determination and nerve-control' – to the extent of qualifying as a First Class Shot. I thoroughly enjoyed it, but always regretted that I didn't qualify as A Marksman – that would have entitled me to wear on my sleeve a badge consisting of a rifle with a star above it. Now that would have been something!

Part of learning to shoot, of course, was being taught to set an aim. One soldier would lie on the ground facing another who was holding a rifle. The one without the rifle would hold a metal disc about two inches in diameter on a nine-inch pin – a little like a lollipop. This 'lollipop' had a small aperture at the lowest central portion of the aiming mark. Through this the lollipop-bearer could check on the accuracy of aim of his companion. We also had firing practice on the miniature range in the gymnasium. We fired from a distance of 25 yards with a .22 calibre rifle at targets. There were three forms of target: a standard one represented a large size target at 100 yards. Such a firing-range would, of course, be outdoor and the calibre of rifle would be .303 – the standard Lee Enfield army rifle. The next target was a difficult thing to score on – being about half the size of the standard. Finally, there was the 'snap' target. It was on a stalk about three inches in diameter and was lifted up for a certain number of seconds for each of the five shots which the competitors would fire. The chaps were of varying abilities when it came to firing. A fellow who could conjugate French irregular verbs could not necessarily hit a target at all! Nobody was allowed to advance from the firing point until each of the four shooters had fired his five rounds. After the last round was fired, the command would be given to collect targets and bring them back for inspection by the officer commanding the range. How well I remember the disappointment on the faces of those who advanced upon their targets and found them completely unscathed! There was the temptation to indulge in a little raw work with a sharp instrument on the way back for inspection! My own expertise with a rifle – as it turned out – stood me in good stead many, many years later in a story which involved pigeons and stained glass windows! More of that in a future chapter of my life.

CHAPTER VI

The Musical Years

During my time with the OTC my musical career enjoyed something of a revival. I had always been interested in blowing into things to get notes out of them – those of you who are paying attention will remember the swap involving the harmonica and the piano accordion, which admittedly you don't blow, but wind is involved! To this day, in the absence of an instrument, I am something of a whistler – a habit of which I am not always aware, and which sometimes causes annoyance to those around me! The great opening offered me in the OTC band was blowing a bugle. Soon I was established among the chaps who were allowed up a little staircase into the Band Room (for that is what it was called) where other boys were frantically drumming on tables with drumsticks or blowing into muted bugles.

Shortly after my joining the Corps of Drums as a bugler, fifes were introduced. Every bugler was also expected to function on the fife, the little flute. I had never dreamed of the opportunities this was to open up for me. Before very long, an E-Sharp flute was introduced into the proceedings. This was about seven inches longer than the little flute and I was quick to seize the opportunities offered by the larger instrument. Having established myself as competent on the E-Sharp flute I was qualified to provide harmony in the Fife Band. The harmony was entrusted to just two of us. This is because there were only two E-Sharp flutes, and we were up against about twelve chaps blasting out the melody. Whenever we went on route marches across miles of country roads we had to provide music for the marchers to help them to keep step. One of the problems was that, after playing a bugle for a while, you couldn't just switch to the flute: the top lip was settled in the bugle mode and could not readily adjust itself to the far gentler breathing of wind into the much smaller hole near the end of the flute. This meant that, after a stint with the bugle, the marchers had to proceed in step with the aid only of the drummers. Later, when the stiff upper lip had grown somewhat relaxed, the flautists were once again able to join in.

Before very long, when my tentative bugling was rumbled I was given a pair of white gauntlets, a large mace, and four inverted stripes and a silver crown on the lower part of my sleeve. All this indicated that I was the drum major of the outfit. The principle seemed to be that 'if he's no good, give him an executive position' – and how true that can be throughout life. We can all think of people who have been promoted way beyond their capabilities. I successfully held onto the post of Drum Major until I left school and entered the seminary.

CHAPTER VII

The Early Sporting Years

Despite never serving in the Forces, I had the greatest respect and admiration for those who did. I can remember when I was about 17, being on a walk one morning with another boy. We were both in quarantine and living in the College infirmary, as we were suffering from the highly contagious conjunctivitis – otherwise known as 'pink-eye'. After a while on our walk we were aware of an aircraft – a Hurricane fighter from the Polish squadron of the RAF – circling round and getting closer and closer to the ground. Eventually it dipped out of our sight and the engine cut out. We ran up the slope of College Lane until there was a break in the hedge and we saw the Hurricane had attempted to land, but had turned over in a soft, ploughed field. The pilot was trapped between the aircraft and the ground. We ran across the field, and various farmhands followed suit. By dint of exerting pressure under one of the wings we raised the aircraft and were able to pull the pilot free. He was in a pretty poor state as he was taken away to hospital and, sadly, he did not survive. Various bits of the aircraft had shattered and were lying on the ground. Some of these we took as souvenirs of our adventure. Boys will be boys, I suppose you're thinking.

There is a piece of music which always takes me back to those days after France had fallen to the Germans. A French-born boy – his name was Stevens – had arrived at the College about this time. Despite having small hands, he was a remarkably good pianist. All during that hot summer of 1940 he used to play the piano which stood in the School Hall; more often than not it was Mozart that he played – the piece called *Alla Turka*. The doors of the Hall stood open and the sound could be heard all over the Quadrangle, wafting through the heavy heat of the afternoons.

In stark contrast to this summer heat, was the cold of winter. I can't claim that polar bears took up residence in the grounds, but I am sure they would have felt at home if they had. During these war years the College swimming pool was, of course, never heated. It didn't matter so much in the summer, but during the winter it was, frankly, uncomfortable! After our sessions of PT in the gym the quickest way to clean a number of less-than-fragrant boys was to make us plunge into the swimming pool. (We only had six showers and a total of ten minutes before the next lesson!) So we leapt into the pool, grabbing the handrail as we went down so as to leap out again at once. There was no escape as we were supervised by an aristocratic master who sat in gown and mortar board on the diving platform. There was no time for anything but a cursory use of a towel and then the clothes were pulled on to a damp, shivering body. We rushed into class with ties awry and dripping hair and teeth a-chatter. As I mentioned, in summer it was fine. In winter ... you can imagine.

I don't know whether or not it is actually so, but most people of a certain age will declare that winters were colder and summers were hotter in the days of their youth. Certainly I recall the winters being colder than they are today. On the far side of the rugger pitch at St Edmund's there was the Bath Pond. Nobody ever told me why it was called the Bath Pond, and if I had asked why I don't suppose I would have been given any sort of satisfactory reply. It wasn't a very large pond, but in winter time it regularly froze over. This meant that the boys had a ready skating rink. These days, were it to freeze over, there would doubtless be signs all around it warning of the dangers. But in my boyhood we grabbed our skates and rushed on to the ice, with little regard for our 'health and safety'.

In the holidays it was even better: five miles from where I lived was a vast lake – Gosfield Lake – and when it was frozen over it provided literally miles of free skating. I remember leaping on my bicycle, clutching my skates, when I heard it was frozen. It was well worth the cycle ride. Once you broke through the cordon of frustrated and angry swans waiting to bury their heads into your lunch packet, you could race across the ice and leave them all behind, making sure your sandwiches were in your pocket! Accustomed to the limitations imposed upon the keen skater by the dimensions of the Bath Pond, it was sheer joy to speed across the ice at Gosfield with no worries about having to stop suddenly or go round in circles.

As to the summer, towards the end of the war, I recall a series of Harvest Camps which were run by the school at the request of farmers who were looking for labour during the summer holidays. Some of the boys were delighted to find that working on the same farm were Land Girls. Most of these were fairly rough, it has to be said. We were all working on the same farm but the girls and the boys could work separately. I don't think any true romances blossomed out of these brief associations, but it was a diversion for the non-Church boys. The work involved picking up sheaves and standing them on end to form 'traves' – eight sheaves formed one trave, which looked a bit like a tent, the idea being that the sun would dry out the ears of corn as they stood on end, before being collected on carts and carried away to barns, and thence to the miller.

On the whole, my memories of these, my later school days, are reasonably happy. It was not a time of plenty when it came to food, but I loved the rugger and the cricket.

I discovered my love of rugby football at the age of about 16. I played in the First Fifteen for two years. We lost nearly every match in my first year, but in my second, the team was very successful. We lost only once and that was to Ratcliffe College. It was during our winning streak that I found a certain aptitude for the game, and as a result, an enthusiasm. My highest point was in the game against the Perse School, Cambridge when I scored three tries. I played at centre-three-quarter and – although I didn't realise it until my performance was analysed in the school magazine – I appeared to have considerable acceleration; I was not fast over a distance but I was able to take advantage of the gaps in defence which opened up. This love of rugby football was to remain with me to this day, as does the chagrin I feel at never being selected as Captain.

Someone once described rugby football (Rugby Union) as a game for cads, played by gentlemen. (Incidentally, soccer was described as a game for gentlemen, played by cads; and Rugby League was called a game for cads, played by cads! I couldn't possibly comment.) One of the features of rugger is that the referee's word is respected by the players – they don't set about breaking his legs if they disagree with his decisions! I remember watching a World Cup match between, I think, the Irish and the French. There was some sort of an altercation on the field between two opposing forwards. The referee blew his whistle and brought the two miscreants to his side. He pointed at one and said, "You – stop doing that!" And to the other he said, "You – whether he did it or didn't: Rise above it." What a wise referee. And what a wonderful lesson which we could all apply throughout life.

When it came to cricket, strangely, I was appointed captain in my first year in the First Eleven, despite not having even won my colours at that time. I say 'strangely' because I felt I had no natural aptitude for the game. It was when I scored 29 against Bishop's Stortford College that the cricket coach decided to award me full colours. What happened was that our opponents on that day had a very useful leg-break bowler who took the wickets of several of our opening batsmen. I went in to bat at about number 6 and decided that the only way to master this bowler was to move quickly a couple of yards down the wicket and hit him on the half-volley before the turn of his leg-break had a chance to embarrass me. I remained captain for two years; but never made more than fifty runs in an innings. I was not a bowler, but the cricket coach, who bowled a crafty left-arm leg-break, considered me to be a good close-fielder, putting me at short-point or silly mid-off. Both positions were inherently dangerous, but I escaped unscathed apart from once breaking a finger.

Apart from the cricket and the rugger, we also played 'Fives' which was a type of squash played with heavy gloves and no racquet; I was also reasonably able in the boxing ring – obviously drawing on my experience with the malodorous gloves from my childhood! In the boxing tournament I remember having a fierce semi-final bout with a boy called Ian Gilroy. Gilroy was a body-builder but with little talent as a boxer. What he lacked in boxing skill he made up for in rippling physique. It was a fairly close contest but my less-than-rippling physique just won the day! In the final, I met a large boy named Edward Disney. He claimed a kind of distant relationship with Walt, but I don't think anybody believed him. I found the contest much less gruelling than the semi-final, but nevertheless he was declared the winner. That was pretty much the end of my boxing career. Such pugilism was not encouraged in the Seminary where I was shortly to embark upon my philosophy and theology.

CHAPTER VIII

The Seminary – and Am. Dram. Years

I enjoyed my six years in the Seminary. I look back on my time there with joy. There was a lot of laughter, a number of characters and many, many wise lessons to be learned from a fine team of professors.

St Edmund's, founded in 1568, is the oldest seminary in England; it enjoys a great reputation as one of the finest Catholic colleges and seminaries in the country – with no fewer than twenty canonised saints in its old registers. After the Reformation, men preparing for the priesthood were sent to France (Douai) or to Rome for training. When the students from Douai in Flanders were able to return to this country, it was to Old Hall Green that they went. There they were received into a small school established by a man whose name, I think, was Mr Pottinger, and that was the beginning of St Edmund's College, near Ware in Hertfordshire.

The seminary was connected to the school buildings by a narrow passage. We shared the use of the Pugin-designed chapel; but converse between pupils and what we called the 'Divines' was forbidden.

As I have already mentioned, I loved being in the seminary. The principal relief was to be free of the close supervision and multiplicity of rules which obtained in the school. I was by now 18 years of age and it was time to start studying seriously to become a priest. We had a large lecture hall divided into two sections – one for philosophers and the other for theologians. I can't say that I really ever enjoyed philosophy. I had only the vaguest ideas of the concepts with which we were presented. One branch I remember clearly was called Epistemology. It was the science of the absorption of knowledge. Another branch was Logic. The latter was supposed to teach you how to present arguments (usually theological) in an ordered fashion. I never really understood Epistemology, but it didn't seem to matter much. To digress slightly onto the subject of sneezing (there is a point to this), you are probably familiar with the fact that, supposedly, every time you sneeze a number of brain or memory cells (I can't remember which!) are supposed to be destroyed. I am an enthusiastic 'sneezer' (my sneeze on one occasion being compared to a dog fight, of all things!). But on this particular occasion I remember walking out of the refectory behind the diminutive figure of John Harper-Hill. He was an amusing character; quite a serious person when it came to study. I heard an explosive crash in front of me and it was the sound of a huge sneeze from the same diminutive character. It was a really hearty sneeze, and as he blew his nose afterwards he muttered, "There goes my Epistemology". As we were then approaching exam-time, his was a serious condition! Fortunately, he managed to pass all his examinations and was duly ordained two years later.

For the next few years there seems, in retrospect, to have been a variety of unusual people coming and going in the Seminary. The main body of students remained the same: it was just that the number of "transients" seemed to me to be unusually large. This was a time when people were returning from the Forces and so we saw an extraordinary collection of more mature men joining the community. There was Edward Lingard. He was a very polished ex-naval officer who had accompanied Princess – now Queen – Elizabeth on her journey to South Africa. He was a fine man, but the victim of scruples. Eventually it led him to leave the Seminary, and I felt that the Church had lost an excellent potential priest. Years later I came across him as a patient in the Edward VII Hospital for Officers in Marylebone. He was then living in Surrey and had been laid low by a heart defect.

One day an unfortunate fellow – hollow eyed and cadaverous – joined the community. He was promptly – and cruelly some might say – dubbed Lazarus. So, from the time he arrived, he was given little chance. He was pedantic and without much humour and I would have guessed that he would not stay the course. He didn't.

Another character I remember from those days was called Aidan Daniel. He was named Bebe – almost after the cabaret artiste, who performed with Ben Lyon. Bebe was angular and slightly aristocratic (he'd been at Downside). He was clever and without much humour, and scruples took him out of the Seminary, too. Later he became a doctor of medicine. From all of this you might begin to form the opinion that a sense of humour is just about as important as a sense of devotion when it comes to the priesthood – and indeed, life in general – although maybe that is only the writer's opinion. It seems to me that some of the finest and best-loved priests I have ever known have been able to laugh at themselves and at life. As we read in Ecclesiastes, – paraphrase – "there is a time for tears and a time for laughter." And that, dear reader is the first – and quite possibly the last, who can tell – scriptural quote to occur in this opus!

Apart from all the studying – which was not terribly demanding, I reckoned anyway, there was plenty of time for sport and Amateur Dramatics. The system in the Seminary was for a student to be appointed 'Chairman of Concerts'. His responsibility was to make sure that a few 'turns' would be assembled for the various Common Room concerts which took place three or four times a year. Apart from that, there were the main dramatic productions which occupied a good deal of our time in the months preceding Christmas and Easter. I was given the lofty position of Chairman of Concerts one year and I remember producing a comedy (surprise, surprise!): a joint production by Ian Hay and P G Wodehouse. I have a feeling it was called "Leave it to Psmith"; certainly it included a character called Mr Bassington-Bassington. My memory is that it was far more fun for the 'actors' taking part, than for the audience – but then that might always be the case when it comes to 'Am. Dram.'!

When I wasn't Chairman, I took part in many a production. I had the very interesting part of Mr Meister – a character who was a keen pianist – in "The Amazing Dr Clitterhouse"; I also played a barrister on one occasion, and an army officer called Captain Stanhope in "Journey's End". I loved amateur dramatics and had no trouble at all in learning my lines. I was nearly always given a prime part in the non-musical productions, and lesser roles in the musicals! Who knows, if I had not gone in for the priesthood, I may well have been surrounded by Oscars by now!! Or not.

CHAPTER IX

A Time of Change

The holidays from the Seminary were the same length as the school holidays. Whilst I was a pupil in the school, I had always been reluctant to return to St Edmund's after my weeks at home; but once I had started at the Seminary, I was always quite happy to return. I suppose that shows how much I loved my time in the seminary. It was full to bursting all the time and there was an excellent spirit there.

When I did go home for the holidays I was not idle. One way of raising some money was to go to the Pershore/Malvern area and tear our fingers to tatters pulling unripe plums from the trees. I should explain that this was not some form of illegal scrumping on my part – I was actually being gainfully employed by jam-makers who paid us to pick the plums – which had to be unripe for their purposes. Unripe plums do not relinquish easily their attachment to mother tree: hence the tattered fingers. It hasn't put me off plum jam, strangely; that is still one of my favourites. While we performed this plum-picking task we were given digs in the homes of the locals; I am still in touch to this day with one of my host families.

The greater part of my holidays was spent at home. My younger sister, Pat, was about 10 or eleven years old by now, and was attending the convent school in Essex where I had been a pupil before I went to St Edmund's. The school was still being run on a shoe-string by Franciscan Sisters. It was mainly to provide a Catholic education for children of the area. Boys and girls came in from as far a-field as Finchingfield and Witham because there were no other Catholic schools in the area of East Anglia. The school was so well run that non-Catholic parents sought places for their children. It was understood that fees were charged for these pupils – one guinea per term.

Pat loved her time at the convent, and clearly took her religious education very seriously. Having learned in the RI class that anyone could baptise in an emergency, she took her friend Joan Mary Webb, into the convent chapel at the end of school one day, removed the dripping sponge from the holy water stoop, and baptised Joan Mary Webb a Catholic, something which, in the strictest sense, cannot be reversed unless the subject abjures the Faith. The nuns were horrified when they discovered what had happened, but common sense soon prevailed, and no one worried too much about the event – except Pat, who still remembers the occasion and has some misgivings about her role as a latter-day female John the Baptist.

It was while I was at the seminary in 1946 that my father died in hospital of cancer, at the age of 64. He had lost his job at Crittalls because he had taken a stand on a matter of principle. Father had then taken up work for the government of the day. His job was to travel around locally to assess people who had applied for National Assistance. This he did on his bicycle, often riding many miles over the course of a day. On one occasion he had to cross a railway line at a level crossing. The main gates were closed and pedestrians could pass through the swing gates to cross the track. My father pushed his bike out from this swing gate, failing to notice an approaching train on that line. The train struck his cycle and severed a finger on his right hand, which was holding the handlebars. I have always thought that this accident provoked the cancer which was soon after diagnosed in my father, and eventually led to his premature death. RIP.

Shortly after their move to Braintree, my parents had bought a small general groceries shop, which my mother ran almost single-handedly. She was much loved in the area and people used to come in and discuss their problems with her. After my father's death, my mother continued to run the shop, before my eldest brother induced her to leave Braintree where there were constant reminders to her of my father. As it turned out, it was an ill-judged action, because what Kevin arranged was a house in Hounslow, Middlesex to which mother moved in 1947. Kevin could not possibly have foreseen how much my mother would miss the advantages of living in a small town. Hanworth, the precise part of Hounslow to which she went, was a residential part of the town, not far from Twickenham. My sister, Pat, of course, was only about 12 when she went with my mother to their new home. She had to change schools, and was never very happy at the 'new' school she had to attend.

CHAPTER X

Charlie

I, meanwhile, was continuing my studies at the seminary. It was the place where many enduring friendships were forged. There are a number of people alongside whom I studied who are still friends to this day. One such – Charles McGowan – became a venerable canon of the Diocese of Westminster. And also a bit of a fighter! On one occasion he and another student were waiting outside the room of our Scripture Professor. The said professor was a very dull lecturer, but a much sought-after Confessor. Charles and the other student – a pugnacious man called Denis McGuinness – fell to wrestling (McGuinness was a confirmed wrestler with anybody). Both were in cassocks as we all had to be in the house, and both were wearing birettas. During their exchanges the birettas became separated from their heads and were kicked around the floor as McGuiness struggled to throw McGowan to the ground. The scuffle caused the Scripture Professor to open his door and survey the scene, "You should be wearing your birettas," he said, by way of rebuke, before closing his door again – apparently ignoring the fact that two cassocked chaps had each other in some sort of stranglehold on the floor.

Charles McGowan and I much later ended up in the same retirement home. Charlie, God rest him, remembered little in his last days but he did remember That Scuffle. It is one of a couple of things Charlie remembered – the other being the Incident with The Golf Clubs. Still vivid in his mind when he arrived at St Peter's retirement home was that Cardinal Cormac

Murphy-O'Connor had purloined three of his golf clubs. Allegedly. This rankled bitterly with the Canon to his dying day. He didn't play golf latterly of course, but that mattered little! One of these days I must give the Cardinal the right of reply – it seems only decent before his name is thoroughly blackened. To pinch a chap's golf clubs is one thing; to pinch a Scottish chap's golf clubs can only be regarded as foolhardy! P G Wodehouse has a lovely expression: "It is never very difficult to distinguish between a ray of sunshine and Scotsman with a grievance". I always think of Charlie as "a Scotsman with a grievance" in this situation.

Charlie was also a very resourceful man. Visiting a class one day in the parish school, he asked the children what they had been studying. They replied, "The Acts of the Apostles" – in particular the bit where Philip jumps up onto the chariot and tries to explain the Scriptures to the eunuch of Queen Candace. To Charlie's dismay, one canny pupil asked him, "Sir, what's a eunuch?" Charlie pondered this for a moment and then said, bravely, "A eunuch, my boy, is a servant. A trusty servant. A verrrry trusty servant." (Imagine it with a Scottish accent!)

CHAPTER XI

Catering – and More Scots

My time in the Seminary was, for the most part, a time of shortage. Bread was rationed, even though the war was over and there were still many other shortages wished upon us by Stafford Cripps, who, like the good Evangelical he was, made sure that the starving people of Europe were fed, even though it meant rationing food in the UK. In desperation, I developed a method of heating water to make cocoa. It involved dismantling batteries, and using some of the component parts in conjunction with the mains electricity to heat cups of water. I can go into no more detail now for fear of encouraging others to experiment in what was, frankly, a hazardous operation. To the hot water we added powdered milk and cocoa and sugar. The operation, if carried out in a particular fashion, would produce a nice head of foam on the cocoa. The Cocoa Club was called the Crooked Spoon. This reminds me that an astute fellow student from Northampton, Anthony Dillon, a very gifted young man (who later died tragically in a motor cycle accident) had set himself up as a kind of arbiter of excellence among the catering centres in the seminary. He and his two cronies would announce his intention of visiting your establishment – Egon Ronay-style – and issuing one of his worthless Certificates of Excellence. I possess mine to this day. My catering career was to see a revival at University – and again upon retirement!

During my time in the Seminary there was one period when Scottish Bishops began to send their students to be trained there. The influx of the Scots enriched the community hugely. Years later I recall being in Thurso – the last place before the Orkneys on the north coast of Scotland. The parish priest there at the time was Fr Bernard McDonald. On my first visit to Thurso in about 1993, I took him out to lunch. It was then that he told me how much the Scottish students had relished the opportunity to study and spend time in Allen Hall – the name of the seminary part of St Edmund's College.

In all I was to spend twenty-four years of my life at St Edmund's – eleven as a student, then a gap of three years, before returning as a member of staff. That gap of three years was taken up at Cambridge University, but before that there was a very important event in my life.

CHAPTER XII

Early Priesthood – and Sermons

It was on 16th July 1950 that I was ordained in the college chapel at St Edmund's. Mine was a small year. Only six of us were presented for ordination that year. The reason for the small number of candidates was that some of the people in my year were called up for military service; at least one was killed in action and another did not return to the seminary to continue his studies for the priesthood. Those of us who were ordained received the priesthood from Cardinal Bernard Griffin, Archbishop of Westminster. My family attended the ordination and were lodged in the upper part of the rood screen. This gave them a fine view of the whole sanctuary, with the organist in his position just behind them. At the end of the ordination, all the *ordinati* processed to the ante-chapel where we stood to give our first blessings to family and friends and boys in the school who had attended the ceremony. My father had died in 1946; but my mother and three brothers and two sisters were present. Afterwards the family and I went out to lunch in a nearby hostelry, and I began to try and get accustomed to being called Father Miles.

One of my first duties – about two weeks into my priesthood was to officiate at the marriage of my second brother, Paddy to Cynthia Sparks. Cynthia was not then a Catholic, so the ceremony was very low key – as it was in those days at mixed marriages: there was no organ, no hymns, no sermon and no flowers. A couple of years later I instructed Cynthia in the Catholic faith and she was received into the Church, to which she has remained faithful ever since.

I mentioned that there was no sermon. Many people are surprised to learn that, during our time in the Seminary, amidst lectures in theology, philosophy, scripture and liturgy there was no set programme to teach us how to preach or deliver a sermon. Common sense would tell any student in the seminary that he ought to join one of the several 'sermon clubs' which had grown up. In these clubs we would be obliged to preach a formal sermon to the members of the club from time to time. At each meeting there would be a formal sermon and then a kind of 'emergency' sermon preached by one member who, at the start of the meeting would be given a slip of paper which said, "You are to preach on the following text ...". This was to give us practice in quasi-off-the-cuff preaching. In addition one was required to preach at least one 'Public Sermon'. You would be given half a term or so to prepare for this occasion. You could have a script about your person, but you were not permitted to read it – only refer to it.

The keener theologians in our midst were in a high state on these occasions, hunting for heresy. In the post mortem which followed the sermon they would fall upon the unfortunate preacher with enthusiasm if they had detected such a thing! At the end of the public sermon, we were invited by the staff present to offer any comments. The staff would offer theirs. Finally, the wretched preacher would be brought back to face the music. This was orchestrated by the staff, who told him all the bitter things that had been said about his sermon – and added their own comments too. It was not quite as formidable as it appears. In fact, it was quite exhilarating to have one's amateurish efforts graced with such attention from theologians (among the staff) and theologians and philosophers among the students. The preacher on these occasions was always rather formal, and the exercise was stiff. By contrast, an ex-Anglican clergyman who had joined us in the Seminary stood up and preached without reference to script and with great aplomb. How I envied him! He was so relaxed and confident and preached really well. I think it is safe to say that the bulk of our training in preaching took place 'on the job'.

I have already mentioned Canon Charles McGowan earlier in these ramblings, and speaking about sermons reminds me how, on one occasion, the same Canon pointed out to me a verse from one of the psalms in Sunday Vespers. The verse was, "He shall drink from the stream by the wayside, and therefore he shall lift up his head." "What the dickens does that mean?" asked Charlie. "Canon," I said, "you have criticised the holy word. I suspect your purgatory will consist of a long line of pulpits, up the steps of which you will be obliged to go. When you arrive in the pulpit you will find a note: your sermon is on this topic: 'He shall drink from the stream by the wayside, and therefore he shall lift up his head.' Do your best!" To be perfectly honest, I have to say that I have not the slightest idea of the significance of this passage! They didn't teach me that in the Seminary and I never had the nous to ask the Scripture Professor about it!

I was expecting that, after my ordination, I would be appointed to a parish, as the other five candidates had been. I had visions of a little country village parish with roses around the presbytery door and with me knowing everyone in the village by name. In the event, I was told that I could take on supply work (standing in for another priest) wherever I wished. In October I would have to present myself at the University of Cambridge. This was the wish of the diocesan authorities who wanted me to return to St Edmund's and teach on the staff as a fully qualified teacher. In a way, I was delighted to go to Cambridge: it meant that I could continue to play rugger (!) and I didn't mind the prospect of returning to the familiar surroundings of St Edmund's as a teacher.

CHAPTER XIII

The Rugger Years

Priests who went up to Cambridge could be accommodated at St Edmund's House. This House had been set up in Cambridge by Westminster Diocesan authorities – it had nothing to do with the Seminary, but the Rector of the House could always ensure that priests coming in to live there would be accepted in one of the University Colleges – usually Christ's. About forty of us (priests from all dioceses in England and Wales) lived and ate there. Each of us was also a member of one of the constituent colleges of the University. Christ's was my college. I went there for supervisions, (tutorials they are called in Oxford) and had to dine in Hall one night a week. We had to wear short undergraduate gowns at lectures, at supervisions and whenever we were in the town after dark.

St Edmund's House was some little distance out from the city centre and we all had bicycles for going in to lectures. I was reading English for the first two years, switching to history in the third. All my lectures took place in Mill Lane where there were large lecture halls. In my first year we had no supervisor in English at Christ's; so we all went to the rooms of Dr F R Leavis, a don of Downing College and a very popular lecturer. Leavis quarrelled with all his colleagues in the English Faculty, denouncing most of them; but he never made a student, however foolish (as I was in terms of English Literature) feel inadequate.

Of course the real joy of being at Cambridge was ... the rugger! I remember in the first Christ's trials of the season I was carted off the field with an injured back. I was very anxious to get back into the game, but the Captain (one of my helpers as I left the field) assured me, "Don't worry, we know what you can do – there's no need for you to go back on." I was given a place in the 1st XV. This was largely on the strength of my having played for London Irish 1st XV during the vacations from the Seminary.

Rugger as a game is notorious for the injuries it can inflict on its participants. Fortunately I rarely sustained any serious injuries in the game. Well, I suppose you don't if you stay well away from the scrum. I did stay away from the scrum and always played in the three-quarter line. A broken finger and a minor concussion were the sum total of my afflictions. The peculiar thing about being concussed is that, although you don't really know what is going on around you, or why these people keep coming towards you aggressively, you can still go on doing more or less the right thing almost as if you were on auto-pilot. I can't say that I ever actually crossed the line in a concussed state, but I know that I didn't disgrace myself when I went on playing after a concussion. The present wisdom is that anybody who has been concussed should not be allowed to continue with the game until he has fully recovered, but in my day I was taken to the side-line for about 5 minutes, and then allowed to resume. In a slightly bemused state, but still doing more or less the right thing, I asked a colleague on the field, whom we were playing and what the score was. Anyone who has been concussed will know how the short-term memory is so impaired you forget something as soon as you hear it. I remember that I kept on asking the chap next to me the same questions –'who are we playing and what's the score?'

Actually those weren't the only injuries. Now that I come to think of it, I also sustained a fractured shoulder blade, which took about six weeks to heal itself. Furthermore, I lost my ability to sing falsetto – or any high notes at all – when I tackled a chap who was trying to get away from me with the ball. As I threw myself at his lower limbs, one of his booted feet came up and kicked me heartily in the throat. He couldn't help it: he was just running. I shouldn't have tackled him so enthusiastically.

Speaking of injuries, I think the single most painful thing that happened to me occurred many years later. It was not long before my 80th birthday, when I foolishly decided to try and ride a new bicycle which I had given to my sister, Pat, for her birthday. I was alright while I was on the straight. Then I tried a 'u' turn – and the bike and I parted company. I fell heavily and managed to bruise seriously several ribs. Nothing can be done about that sort of injury, of course. You just have to be patient and wait for the bruising to subside. But the pain really is intense. Merely breathing in a particular way can cause great yelps of pain! If you have ever experienced bruised or cracked ribs, you have my unadulterated sympathy. But I digress again; back to Cambridge.

By this time I was altogether consumed with a passion for the game of rugger. I well remember how, on one occasion, I had been writing a history essay in the morning. It was due to be handed in at 5pm when I went in to College for a Supervision. I wrote as much as I could in the morning, broke off to have a quick lunch, returned to the essay, but did not finish it before it was time to get on my bike and cycle to Christ's rugger pitch. The match was played in rather muddy conditions; I had no time to wait for a shower (my essay being unfinished). I arrived back at St Edmund's House and, abandoning all thoughts of shower or tea, wrote a bit more essay. At 4.55pm I leapt on my bike to go down to college. The essay was unfinished, but I knew what the last paragraph was going to say. I arrived at college, my tutor – Professor Jack Plumb – called me in and asked me to read my essay. This I did – with increasing trepidation as I approached the final page. Keeping my eyes fixed on the paper I recited the final paragraph as it had been in my memory. Happily he did not ask to see the written effort. I am pretty sure he never realised that the script was incomplete. This tendency of mine to brinkmanship was to haunt me later in life in my days as a parish priest, when, on occasions, I could be found hurtling down the stairs of the Rectory with the last paragraph of my Sunday sermon uncommitted to paper!

Remembering the episode of the muddy knees and Professor Plumb brings to my mind the whole business of keeping one's rugger kit clean. At day-school, of course, this unenviable task usually fell to the poor mother of the sportsman; at university the situation was slightly different – especially in the days before launderettes. However, my salvation was the Cambridge Steam Laundry to which I handed in, after every match, my muddy rugger gear. Returning to the Laundry one day to pick up my clean gear, the items were put in front of me – shirt, shorts, stockings – but one item was missing: personal, but vital. To be frank and not wishing to offend your sensibilities, the jock strap was absent. I enquired of the kindly lady behind the counter about the missing item, and she went on a tour of the Laundry calling out loudly, "Has anyone seen the Reverend Miles's jockstrap?" The result of her paging was the arrival of one lady triumphantly swinging the missing item. This has always remained in my mind: the only occasion on which I was paged for my jockstrap.

This incident to do with cleaning, reminds me that, many years later, when I was a parish priest at Spanish Place in London, I took my cassock to Sketchley's to be dry-cleaned. When I went to pick it up, the assistant asked the manageress, "Was it a hassock?" "No, she replied, "it's a kossack." The matter was debated for a while before I gently sorted it out for them.

Before we leave the delicate subject of gentlemen's personal protective sportswear I must record the visit of an Austrian schoolmaster – Dr Ernst – who was temporarily on the staff of St Edmund's. One afternoon, he was persuaded to join in with a game of cricket, despite the fact that he had no experience whatsoever of the game. When it came to his turn to bat he emerged from the pavilion with white shirt, dark flannels – and a gleaming white cricket box strapped on the *outside* of his trousers. He successfully negotiated deep square leg but was smartly collared by mid-on and escorted back to the pavilion where certain adjustments to his dress were suggested. No more box or jock strap stories – I promise.

To return to Cambridge and the rugger, I suppose the zenith of my rugger career came in 1952, when Christ's arrived at the final of the university Cuppers' Competition. This was a knockout competition involving all the colleges of Cambridge University in the Lent term. It was a major event, the highlight of the rugger player's year, the final of which was played on the University rugger ground at Grange Road. Our opponents in the final were Pembroke College. One of the things that remain vividly in my mind is the vociferous and spectacular enthusiasm of Christ's supporters. They made such a show that we couldn't even countenance the possibility of losing! Shortly after the beginning of the match a Pembroke centre sped through to score a try under our posts. We were 5-0 down. It stayed like that until the second half when our Welsh outside-half, Derek Iles, landed a drop-goal. Shortly after that we got the ball moving down our line and I broke through under the posts for our kicker to convert; we were now 8-5 up. I can't remember much more about the game, but I know that we did score another try which was converted and we WON 13-5. Our supporters in the stands erupted at the close. That evening, in Hall, the Master of Christ's spoke before the meal and the grace. "We congratulate the Christ's Rugby Football XV on winning the University Cuppers – for the first time in 400 years." The excitement and joy at being part of this achievement was almost immeasurable for me.

The following year we survived only two rounds of the competition before being knocked out. In that year I was Captain. At the rugger dinner at the end of term, I sent my menu card round the table, and when it came back to me, one of the forwards had written along the top "Sorry the bullocking forwards let you down". I suppose we had all expected to win the Cuppers a second time; but it was not to be.

The 1952 team is still reunited at Christ's every five years to celebrate and remember our victory. We have a champagne party in the Fellows' Garden, followed by dinner in Hall. With the passing years our numbers have depleted, of course, but there are still sufficient of us to meet again and relive the glories of 1952. Rugger players have long memories!

CHAPTER XIV

More Cambridge – and Rugger

Believe it or not, there was more to my time at Cambridge than just the rugger! I had to produce essays at regular intervals and to study for examinations each year! At the end of my time in the English Faculty I switched to History. My supervisor in English understood my inclination to make the switch; but I remember his saying, when he told me the result of my final Tripos Examination in English, "Yes, you did get a third, but it was within hailing distance of a 2-2." I clung on to that guarded congratulation fiercely – and remember it clearly to this day – as you can tell.

One of my abiding recollections of my one year in the History Faculty was of my Supervisor coming to lunch at St Edmund's House on the Sunday preceding the start of the examinations. After lunch he walked around the grounds with me and I took the opportunity to ask questions on various aspects of the History course I had completed with him. In such ways were some of my deficiencies covered up. In the finals I was given a 2-2. Not a great degree, but a degree which enabled me to put MA (Cantab.) after my name. And also to enjoy my rugger-playing!

I loved my time at Cambridge and still keep in touch with some of my rugger colleagues from those days. I do think that a university education should be a lesson in life's experiences, and not just three years of academic slog. People should come away having worked hard, played hard and learned how to be more confident and resourceful human beings, ready to take their place in society. Not that I necessarily had done this – but I do believe that people should! So runs my theory!

Apart from the rugger, – and the occasional essay – there was plenty of fun and laughter. I remember going into college on the morning following the rugger dinner in 1953. I called on the secretary to find out if all had gone well (I had left the company at about 9.45pm in a saintly fashion to return to St Emund's House). The Secretary said in his rather melancholic Scottish way, "We had trouble last night, Fred. Jim Roberts poured beer on the Proctor."

The Proctor that term was Dr Prest, a don and tutor at Christ's. The Proctor was the university don responsible for discipline. He normally did his rounds of the city accompanied by two Bullers. These were large men in navy blue suits and bowler hats and very fleet of foot. I remember being very impressed when I heard that Bullers, before reporting a subject for interrogation by the Proctor, would say to the miscreant, "Are you a member of this University?" If he answered in the affirmative, the Proctor would fine him 13/4d (approximately 67 pence in today's money) if his offence was, for example, not wearing a gown after dark, or smoking in the street. If he denied that he was a member of the university, the Bullers would make further enquiries, and if they discovered that the student was being economical with the truth, would report him to his College and he would be sent down. There was no escape.

To return to the beer-pouring incident – it appeared that Jim Roberts, a rugger Blue who later played for England – had leaned out of a first floor window and poured beer on people below. Little did he know that among the people below were the Proctor and his two Bullers, returning after their disciplinary tour of the city. It seems that the Senior Tutor, Dr Pratt, had told Robin Stevenson, a Scot and our Secretary in

1953, that he must apologise to Dr Prest for the indignity he had suffered. I asked Robin, later, how he had got on with the grovelling apology. "Dr Prest I've tae apologise on behalf of the Rugby Club. I understand that you had beer poured on you last night from a first floor window." The wonderfully donnish answer was, "Oh, it was the Rugby Club was it? I thought it might be somebody pouring beer *privately*". It seemed that because it was not a 'private' pouring, that he was totally understanding of the situation.

It was not all beer-pouring and high-spirited jinks. There was a good deal of late-evening coffee-drinking too. In our house of residence, it was a practice for half a dozen of us to gather together to drink coffee at 9.45 pm. On one particular evening, a notable absentee was Fr Tom Rhatigan. Jack Scarisbricke said that he had heard that Tom had been summoned to the Rector's room. The Rector was Canon Corboy. "Well, we must get him out," declared Lord William Taylour, a regular member of the coffee-drinking fraternity. With an enamel mug in his hand, he strode determinedly from the room, went along to my room (adjacent to the Rector's) and hammered on the hot water pipe, knowing that this would be heard in Canon Corboy's room and that Fr Rhatigan would know the significance of the reminder. The mug-banging worked, and Tom appeared to relate that the good Canon Corboy had almost jumped out of his seat when the pipes had clanged.

During the Easter vacation of 1953, when I was captain of the Christ's XV rugger team, we went on a tour of south Wales. Our first two matches brought us comfortable wins; but the third match was a rather tougher affair and we were beaten by a small margin. A young boy rushing on to the pitch afterwards for autographs told me, "You'll have to go home and get some more practice" (how I wish I could write in a Welsh accent). After this match we repaired to a local hostelry, in the basement of which were the showers used by the local rugger club. I was rather slower than most in removing the mud and eventually I emerged from the basement and moved up to the reception room at the top of the pub, where people were drinking beer. I said to one of the Welshman, "Where did they get all this beer?" He told me they had picked it up at the bar on the way up. I told him I had missed out on that, and then remarked that there was a pint of beer on a ledge behind him. "If you want it, you have it," he said. So I took it. Later on our club secretary, who had been talking to the secretary of the Welsh side in the middle of the room, confided in me that the Welshman had remarked, with his jaw dropping, "I don't mind him pinching my beer, but a vi-car ..." (how I really do wish I could write with a Welsh accent).

CHAPTER XV

The Teaching Years – and Howlers

Immediately after being awarded my degree at Cambridge, I did some supply work in the parish of Hampton-on-Thames. It was delightfully situated beside the river, and I soon got to know the charming people who made up the parish. After about three months there I was recalled to St Edmund's college to take up my post as teacher of English at 'A' and 'O' level and French and Latin in the lower forms of the school. Teacher training was in its infancy, as far as graduates were concerned, and (whisper it) I had no such training. I had signed on for some teacher training at Cambridge – largely because it would have meant a continuation of my rugger-playing days. But in the event, Cardinal Griffin came to visit Cambridge and told me that I would have to start teaching at St Edmund's the following September, 1953. And one didn't argue with Cardinals.

Teaching was easier in those days – especially, perhaps, at such a school. There was no real difficulty with classroom discipline, but if you were one yard behind the pupils, you did not have an easy time. Some of the lay masters let the boys get the better of them, and suffered as a result. Fortunately I never had any problems; I think I was regarded as 'firm but fair' – well, certainly firm, and I hope, fair. Many, many years later a former pupil stated that I had been 'demanding' as a teacher. I suppose I should be grateful for the fact that the boys referred to me outside the classroom by the shortened version of my first name. A colleague of mine at that time was less lucky. His surname began with 'K' and in the interests of alliteration he was dubbed 'Killer Kelly'. It's true that he was autocratic in dealing with the boys, and this was duly noted. Mind you, in those days, caning was still common-place for miscreants. This was administered by House-Masters, one of which I became in 1962 until my departure from the school in 1966. When I was a scholar I was caned only twice, to the best of my memory; I didn't care for it and quickly decided that the game was not worth the candle.

In my days as a caning House-Master, I was frequently called upon to administer the cane – and sometimes with monotonous regularity to the same boys. I can remember one in particular who was for ever in trouble and presenting himself in my office for punishment. He was an engaging character who took his beating manfully, showed no signs of ill-will and always thanked me politely as he left the room. I met him quite recently – and he still bears me no ill-will!

I can only remember – with some horror – once reducing a lad to tears. It was as a result of his French homework. When he presented himself at my desk to collect his marked exercise book, I pointed out the plethora of red marks and crosses all over the pages. "What are you going to do about all of this?" I demanded. To my dismay, his 14year-old eyes welled up with tears as he tentatively suggested that he might "Improve". I feel guilty about that episode to this day, and I pray that I did not scar the lad for life with my unintended severity. French can be tricky for some.

I am not, nor ever have been, a betting man but there was one occasion when I was so sure of my facts that I did lay a small wager. The odds seemed stacked in my favour. It came about when a young lad in my class had written the word 'ancle' to describe the joint between the foot and the leg. I duly circled it in red ink and annotated the margin with 'sp' to indicate a spelling mistake. When the exercise books were handed out in class, the boy put up his hand, "Father, please, why have you circled 'ancle?'. "It's wrongly spelt", I replied. He argued that he thought it was correct. "If you can prove to me that ankle is spelt like that," I said, "I will give you two shillings." (10 pence today – not a lot of money, but a fairly handsome amount back then!). The lad fished about his person and produced quite the scruffiest and most dog-eared dictionary you have ever seen. Turning to the appropriate page, he indicated the word 'ancle' as an alternative spelling for 'ankle'. I paid up. I am not certain but I thought I detected a glint of craftiness behind the wide-eyed innocent look bestowed on me by the lad. I am not quite sure what to make of the fact that that boy went on to become a headmaster!

For any schoolmaster, I suppose one of the highlights of his work is the reading and sharing with his fellow-masters, what are commonly known as Schoolboy Howlers.

One of my favourite exercises was to select examples of some of the words we had encountered during the term, and then ask the boys to use those words in sentences which would demonstrate the correct meaning of the word. For example, being required to use the word 'expurgate', you could say, 'Shakespeare's works have been expurgated so as to make them inoffensive to pious ears'. One lad appeared not to have been paying attention during that lesson when he suggested in his examination answer: "The two old men were expurgating in the valley". One of my colleagues on the staff improved this further when he suggested: "The two old men were expurgating in the alley", which sounds slightly unseemly.

I also remember setting an essay on pets which one lad concluded with a great flourish: "There's no doubt about it, you can always say that the dog is a best man's friend."! I recall reading about a young pupil who wrote an essay on "A bird and a beast". The first part of the essay was on the beast. He dealt with it very thoroughly. "The beast", he said, "has four sides: left, right, back and front. The front is where the head is and the head is for growing horns. The back is arranged for milking." Then he came to the matter of the bird. "The bird I am writing about is a cuckoo. The cuckoo is the most extraordinary bird. It lays its eggs in other birds' nests" – and then he added, with something of a flourish "...and vice versa". We are left to puzzle about what exactly was meant by this. We can only conjecture.

I do remember being mightily impressed by one lad, of about 13 years of age, who was required to give a description of a bicycle. He began, "The bicycle is a peculiar contraption ...". I was so delighted to see the use of the word "contraption", that the lad earned a couple of extra marks. I have reminded him of this on several occasions in his adult life, and we always have a laugh about it.

There was another occasion when in class I asked what the boys' idea of heaven was. A bouncy English boy said, "Well, you don't actually do anything; you just sit round and feel smashing." A sad-faced South American boy, when asked for his opinion said, "Is the only place you can be without any molestation." The boy in question (Rappaccioli) was once sent to me – I was his Housemaster – by a prefect 'for misbehaviour in the refectory'. I asked the lad about the nature of the 'misbehaviour'. He explained, "The boy next to me was listening to the snap, crackle, pop and I pushed the head in the dish." I was so delighted by this that I could not bring myself to cane the child.

This story is told by a Jesuit father who observed a young boy making regular and frequent visits to the chapel. These sessions did not last very long and he wondered how the lad was passing his time during these visits. One day, the priest asked the boy, "What do you do when you pay your visit to the chapel?" "I make the Stations of the Cross," came the reply. "I see," said the priest, before probing further; "but what do you actually do?" The boy said, "I go round from one picture to the next, looking at them, and each time I say 'Jesus, I am sorry for yer.'" Well, Our Lord Himself told us that there was no need for many words when we pray; there is, no doubt, much to be said for brevity.

Moving from prayers to speeches: after Edmund Hillary with Sherpa Tensing conquered Mount Everest in 1953, I set the boys an exercise in composition. I asked them to imagine that Sir Edmund was to come to the school to talk about the exploit. In preparation for the imagined talk, the boys were asked to compose a vote of thanks for the mountaineer. One lad stood up and delivered his little speech – ending with the words: "And I am sure that I speak for all the boys here when I congratulate Sir Edmund on his big feat."!

That was an imagined visit for the purposes of composition-writing. We did have a real visit from – what we would call today – A Celebrity. A priest of the diocese came down, bringing with him the comedian, Ben Warris, who often starred alongside Jimmy Jewell. On this particular occasion, however, he was accompanied by a British starlet called Susan Shaw. There was a cricket match proceeding as a background for the visit as Ben and Susan wandered around the grounds. It has to be said that Susan, in keeping with her glamorous starlet image, was sporting a pair of very tight trousers. The Headmaster, 'Rex' King, in his usual picturesque style, described the sight of the woman's hind quarters as like "two ferrets in a bag, fighting." It is said that he immediately sought out the bell-ringer and instructed him to ring the bell to call all the boys in to prep. Dangers were obviously lurking with this *femme fatale* on the premises.

I used to love it when I discovered remarks written by other teachers in school reports. One geography master wrote in the report of a boy who obviously did not shine in that subject: "This boy does well to find his way home." Another master once wrote, "My joy at the marked improvement in Williams's handwriting has been somewhat tempered by my shock at discovering the full extent of his inability to spell."

In 1954, at the end of my first term on the staff, two lay teachers (Hugh Strode and Charlie Holmes) and I decided to tour Europe in Hugh's car. It was spacious Morris, but had a nasty habit of back-firing. So my memory of that journey consists of a series of morning exits from French and German towns in which we back-fired our way out of one town after another. I also remember a shopping expedition in a German town. Beforehand it was arranged that I should buy the butter, Holmes should buy the *Marmite* and Strode should get the bread. Hugh checked his dictionary and discovered that bread was *brod*, but when we got into the shop, the whole thing fell apart. Hugh airily enquired of the man behind the counter: *"Haben-sie bruder?"* It surprised Hugh, but delighted me, when the shop-keeper said, *"Jah"*, and called out to the back of the shop, *"Heinrich!"*, whereupon his brother dutifully appeared. In the interests of absolute veracity, I should add that the final part of that story (the bit about Heinrich) is something of a fabrication.

CHAPTER XVI

'Rex'

One of the most striking and colourful people I met at St Edmund's was J H W King, always known as 'Rex', for reasons which should be obvious to the Latin scholar. When I was a pupil there in 1939, he taught mathematics; later he became Bursar. He was also the Commanding Officer of the Officer Training Corps. Obviously, I did not get to know him well while I was a pupil, but he was a highly efficient person and an effective teacher. When I joined the staff in 1953 he was still Bursar. When he discovered that a group of us met every evening at about 9.30 to drink coffee he made a point of calling in on us regularly. He enjoyed the company of priests and when he was about, the craic was always amusing and worth hearing. He was full of anecdotes, garnered from his many years working with schoolboys and their masters, and witnessing the peculiar situations that can develop in any community.

Schoolboys are notoriously remiss in the matter of writing letters home to their parents – unless, of course, they need money. In order to ensure that parents did have regular letters from their sons, it was established as a rule that junior boys would write home every Sunday evening. Their letters then had to be posted, unsealed, through the letter-box of the Housemaster. This was not for any vetting reasons but simply to ensure that the boys had actually written something! It was King who recalled the occasion when a new boy wrote home for the first time. Aged 12, he wrote in a slightly accusing tone

Bridge House, Great Dunmow, Essex. The house where I was born – appropriately enough: in the shadow of the parish church. We lived there for about five years after my parents relocated from Dublin.

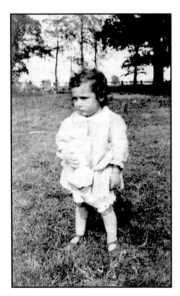

The first photograph of me. I am about 2 years old and not yet "breeched". There were no such things as 'baby-grows' in 1927.

Aged about 6 – already I am holding a ball: a precursor of things to come. The little girl is Margaret Salkeld – who came to stay with neighbours of ours in Bocking.

A day out from St Edmund's –
after swimming in the river.
That's a 'tank top' I'm holding: the
very height of fashion!

My first Holy Communion.
This was taken in the garden of
1, Wordsworth Road: a council
house we lived in between about
1928 and 1934. Signs here of the
'miserable child', I think!

The captain (me) leading my
(I think) victorious team in from a
cricket match at St Edmund's played
against Cheshunt County School.
I am about 17 years old here.
Pretty serious, don't you think?

May 1943. Me as Drum Major in
the Officers' Training Corps, at
St Edmund's. This was after my
lack of skill on the bugle had been
rumbled.

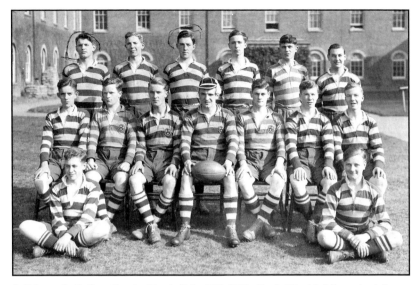

St Edmund's College Rugby Football 1st XV 1942-43. Self is third from the left on the back row. I played Centre-three-quarter.

Circa 1946. Self centre stage 'prosecuting' David Konstant, the now retired Bishop of Leeds. The only time I ever had a bishop in the witness box! He left with unblemished character.

Once more clutching a ball – this time a rugger ball. It's about 1946. Now you see me smile!

Ordination day – 16th July 1950. My first blessing of the boys at St Edmund's.

The Ambulacrum at the seminary.
Left to right: Austin Garvey, Denis Roberts, self, Dan Kay.

Circa 1966. Archbishop's House, Westminster. At this time I was Private Secretary to Cardinal John Heenan.

Sister Anna-Maria with self at Spanish Place. She worked there for about 33 years before returning to her convent. As I write she is just about to reach her 100th birthday.

Examining Papal Blessing from Pope John Paul II on my Golden Jubilee in 2000.

July 2000. My dear sister, Pat, always by my side on important occasions; here, helping me celebrate my Golden Jubilee of Ordination.

In the corridor outside my room at St Peter's on my way down to celebrate Mass for my 80th birthday in 2005. The poinsettia was one of many kind gifts.

At my 80th birthday party to which about 100 very good friends came to help me celebrate. Here I am with Anna and Bunny France: I have known Bunny since 1939 when we were in the same class at St Edmund's.

At the same party – with some of my dear
tennis chums: left to right: Roderic Bullough,
Colin Thubron and Rory McPherson.

Former Captain of Hampshire, the late Colin
Ingleby-McKenzie. Taken at Sir Paul Getty's
magnificent cricket ground in Wormsley,
Oxfordshire. Circa 2002.

Self with my dear friend,
Fran Godfrey (typist of
these memoirs). Taken in
Farm Street Church in
central London in 2003.

Self in retirement – looking un-miserable. I told you I got over being
miserable.

to his parents – who had obviously built up the joys of life in a boarding school. The letter ran: "You said there would be pillow fits (sic); there are none. You said there would be midnight festes (sic); there are none. This is a terrible place. They call bottom arse. Please come and take me home. Your loving son." For all its spelling mistakes, there was a certain rhythmical and poetic quality to it which you cannot fail to admire. This disappointed lad was a contemporary of mine when I was a pupil. He was the slowest fly-half ever to tread on a rugger field, but he gave me, time and again, the most perfect, accurate pass. He was a member of the Colts' XV. On another occasion he wrote home to his parents: "This afternoon I went to play for the Clots (sic) XV against Cheshunt County School. On the way home we stopped in Hoddesdon and I bought a packet of All Brain (sic)." I often wonder what became of him. I have a feeling that he went into farming in Norfolk.

More than one of King's stories centred on Father Smart – 'Boff' Smart, as he was called. He it was who, at the time of public examinations, entered the exam hall and asked to see the School Certificate paper in History, which his boys were about to sit. He then asked the invigilator if he might address the candidates. "This is somewhat irregular, Father, but if it is important ..." "Oh yes it is," replied Boff. With that, he faced his pupils and said, "I've just looked at your exam paper. I find that I have taught you the wrong period. Do your best!" And with that he turned on his heel and left the group of stunned boys to do precisely that. One can only imagine how they managed: 'When one considers the career and achievements of Pitt the Younger, one is quickly struck by their similarity to those of Ethelred the Unready ...'! It is not recorded how well any of the boys did! What is pretty certain is that, today, the school would probably be involved in litigation for such an error. In my life since then, the expression 'Do your best' has come to be used as advice to a person facing an impossible task!

The priest, who taught us history in my time as a pupil, was Father Reginald Butcher. He was a man of very aristocratic manner, but from an impoverished family. In later years (having been headmaster of the Cardinal Vaughan School in Kensington), he came back to St Edmund's as President. Under him, as Bursar, was the afore-mentioned J H W King. The college was always short of money and Mgr Butcher's idea was that the Divines (students in the Seminary) should be made to do work about the place to save the college having to pay labourers. King did not care much for this idea, but dutifully tried to comply with the President's wishes.

On 'President's Gallery', the most prestigious of all galleries, there was, of course, the President's Room, and a place called the Cardinal's room, which the visiting Archbishop of Westminster would occupy when he came to the College. The Bursar persuaded the President that the Cardinal's Room needed re-decorating. "That'll be just the work for Mr Heekin and his fellow-students", said Mgr Butcher. "Well, if you think so", said the Bursar, unconvinced. The work duly went ahead, and on its completion the Bursar, who hadn't at all approved of the scheme of using students for this, announced to the President that the work had been done. "Would you like to see it?" asked the Bursar. He took Mgr Butcher into the freshly decorated room. The good Monsignor looked around and said, "My God! It looks like a brothel!" King's comment in a dry, deadpan, how-would-you-know voice was "Does it Monsignor?"

In 1963 Mgr Butcher suffered a very severe stroke, which landed him in a wheelchair for the last thirteen years of his life. He had been a wonderful schoolmaster and an excellent President. Most evenings I would go along to his room on the President's Gallery to chat to him. I used to rack my brains to think of anything interesting which had occurred during the day and which might divert him. Sometimes it was a question of scraping the bottom of the barrel to dig up something of interest. One half-holiday, a group of boys in my house went to Harlow New Town. It seems they were caught by the police shoplifting in the Co-operative stores. That evening on my regular visit to Mgr Butcher I told him about this incident in the Co-op: "The Co-op?!" said Reggie, obviously appalled. He had always been something of a snob (in the nicest kind of way). I couldn't help thinking that if I had said that the boys had been apprehended in Harrods he might have considered the episode less reprehensible.

We used to be much troubled with stray cats round about the back door of the kitchens. They used to come looking for food. King decided that the only way to get rid of them was to poison them, and brought in a man recommended by the local council. This man's plan was to put out food for the cats and inject it all with strychnine. He explained his tactics to King, who said, "Interesting stuff, strychnine. I understand it gets into the blood stream and paralyses the central nervous system." "No, it don't" came the assured reply, "it poisons 'em." The cats disappeared as if by magic. We would probably never get away with it today! Apologies to cat-loving readers.

Another delightful person who was my contemporary on the teaching staff at St Edmund's was Fr Peter Phillips. He had some endearing idiosyncrasies. He had a tendency to the odd malapropism; he always called the famous savoury sauce, 'Lea & Perkins'. He also had a great ineptitude in respect of the punch-lines in jokes. For example, a simple joke I remember involved the Chinese dentist inviting the patient to come to his surgery. "Two-thirty, alright?" he asked. "Yes, tooth hurtee alright, but when you pullee out?" When Peter tried to relate the joke, he had the Chinaman saying "Half past two alright?" At which point the story fell badly apart. As I said, a delightful man, Peter.

CHAPTER XVII

More Sport!

Of course, you might guess, that my time as a teacher at St Edmund's inevitably involved me in the rugger! First I was given charge of the U/fourteen XV. We had an unbeaten season, after which I took them all down to the local pub in Puckeridge for tea. When we arrived there I surveyed the groaning tables of food which Mrs Macdonald had prepared for the boys. I thought there was enough to feed a regiment, and voiced my concern that there would be heaps of food left over. To which Mrs Macdonald replied, "Have no fear. It will all go." And it did. It was as if a swarm of locusts had been through the room! Well, I suppose they were "growing lads".

The following season, I was put in charge of the first XV. We had a moderately good season. But the next year, we were beaten by only one side: Ratcliffe College. We comfortably beat our principal rivals, Bishop Stortford College and all the others, with that exception. It was a wonderful way to keep my great interest in rugger alive. And all the referee-ing kept me very fit. As far as I know, St Edmund's had never produced an international rugger player for England until the arrival of Jeremy Janion, who went on to play for England round about 1968. As his coach, I was very proud when he achieved international status for England. He was kind enough to say that I had taught him one or two useful tactics in the selling of a dummy and making an opening. And the rugger fans among you will know what all of that means.

Whilst I was coaching rugger, I was invited to the celebration of the Diamond Jubilee of the Rugby Football Union. The gathering took place in marquees at the Twickenham Rugby Ground and the gin and tonic flowed like water, courtesy of the RFU. It was on this occasion that an Irishman, somewhat the worse for drink, lurched over in my direction, enquiring, "Did you ever know the Reverend Robin Rowe? Hooker for Ireland in nineteen hundred and fifty four?" I said I had known him, and he then switched his tack. "Did you ever hear Mario Lanza sing?" "Yes, I have," I replied. "When Mario Lanza died, people in this city wept" he continued. "Where?" I asked, feeling certain that I had put him on the spot. Without so much as a beat pause, he answered, "Tooting." Of all places. To this day I can never think of Tooting without picturing the people en masse on the streets in floods of tears for the loss of Mario Lanza!

Apart from the rugger, I played a bit of cricket. We had a lovely cricket ground at St Edmund's and one of the priests on the staff was mad about the game. It broke his heart when, in mid-July, term ended and we all dispersed, leaving behind an excellent cricket square. It was largely through his inspiration that a Cricket Week was established. Members of staff, some Old Boys and the best two or three boys in the current first XI were invited to come back to the college for a period to play cricket and to play host each day to a different visiting team. This produced some memorable cricket matches. Aside from this, various priests used to arrive at St Edmunds to spend part of their summer vacation. One of these, a French man, was sitting beside me when the cricket teams walked out from the pavilion to start play. Twenty minutes into the game, he turned to me and enquired, "When will zay begin?" I can't say that several wickets had fallen, or that many sixes had been hit: nevertheless the cricket had been proceeding in the fairly customary, static manner! I have heard it said that more calories are burned by the spectators than by the teams: it's a foul slur!

Even more memorable than the games, were the evenings spent in our local hostelry, The Bay Horse with members of the visiting side. The Bay Horse was a fine pub: every evening two or three members of staff would gather there and mingle with the yokels. In would come Wilf Lane, a colourful local character who had a small holding and at least one cow. An old Etonian on his way back from the city to his home in a nearby village would also drop in; there was a wonderful mixture of people from varied walks of life and very different family connections. As you might imagine, the topics of conversation were varied and idiosyncratic! They were happy times.

The continuation of my interest in rugger, the characters I met and the friendships I forged during my thirteen years at St Edmund's made this a fascinating and happy time for me. It was, therefore, a great wrench when I was removed from the school and given a new job.

One year, while I was still on the staff at St Edmund's, and Cardinal Heenan was staying at Hare Street House, quite close to the College, I was deputed by the headmaster to be available one afternoon to play tennis with him on the College courts. About that time the Cardinal would have been entering his sixtieth year, I suppose. I needed to employ all my accuracy of shot to make a game of it; the Cardinal was losing his mobility and I had to put the ball where he was, rather than, as was my wont, to put it where my opponent was not. I suppose that was my first real meeting with the Cardinal; yet, before the year was out, I was in his service at Westminster.

CHAPTER XVIII

The Secretarial Years

So it was, in 1966, that the Vicar-General of the Diocese of Westminster, Bishop Patrick Casey, came down to St Edmund's and told me that I would be leaving at the end of the Christmas term and going to Archbishop's House. The Headmaster was indignant that I should be plucked out in this way in the middle of an academic year when I was teaching 'O' level and 'A' level English. But the decision was out of our hands. It had come about because Monsignor David Norris, the principal private secretary to Cardinal Heenan, had been told that he could select his own assistant. We had known each other at school and in the Seminary, but we were not contemporaries. Nevertheless, for some reason, he thought I would be the man for the job. I was, to be honest, dismayed and highly dubious that it was the sort of work I could do well. In the event, I stayed nine years with Cardinal John Heenan and a little over two years with Cardinal Basil Hume, so I suppose I must have picked it up along the way!

When David Norris became Vicar-General of the Diocese in 1971, I became principal private secretary to Cardinal Heenan, and remained with him until he died in 1975. He did not appoint an under-secretary; so we lived in Archbishop's House alone, apart from the German Sisters who had the top floor.

Unexpectedly, these turned out to be happy times for me. Throughout my life, whenever there has been a change in my situation, I have been hesitant and almost reluctant, to acquiesce. And yet, each time, I have had occasion to be grateful for the decisions that were made for me.

Cardinal Heenan and I hit it off pretty much straight away. I think this might have been in part due to our shared Irish background; it established a ready bond between us. He was also a very able and decisive man whom I admired enormously. He possessed many qualities which I appreciated: he was honest, straightforward and had a great sense of humour. He also had a hatred of the cliché.

Over the years he and I had developed a kind of 'cliché brinkmanship': if he was speaking in public and I was present, he would sometimes approach close to what looked like a cliché and then neatly sidestep it at the very moment I thought he would succumb.

About this time a certain Father Peyton was visiting the British Isles. He was an American priest who was promoting a Rosary Crusade. His slogan (which gained considerable currency at the time) was "The family that prays together, stays together." When I was present at the opening of a school by the Cardinal, he told the children at the end of his address when they went home that evening they should ask their parents to join them in an Our Father, a Hail Mary and a Glory Be. "Because, you know," he said, "the family that prays together" (quick glance in my direction) "will always have God's blessing upon it."! I was sure he was about to fall into the cliché trap; I should have known better.

On another occasion when he was addressing religious sisters of many Congregations in the Cathedral, he said towards the end of his address, "I know that I give thanks to God every day for you; and I am sure you give thanks every day" (glance in my direction) "for the great grace of your vocation."

Not that it was all one-way brinkmanship. We occasionally stayed at Hare Street House – the home of Robert Hugh

Benson, in the area of Buntingford in Hertfordshire. There was a lovely chapel there at the bottom of the garden where Robert Hugh Benson's tomb was situated. Whenever we were there, one or other of us would celebrate Mass in that chapel, which was a Mass centre for people of the district. On this particular occasion the Cardinal was to celebrate Mass in Cambridge later in the day; so it fell to me to celebrate the early Mass at Hare Street. I decided that the game of brinkmanship was too one-sided: so when I was preaching I concluded my sermon by saying, "And you could say that that is what the readings in today's Mass ... emphasise." I couldn't believe at breakfast how easily he had fallen into the trap because, instead of seeing that I had deliberately set this up, he enquired kindly whether, if he had not been present, I might have said, "and that is what the readings in today's Mass are all about." "I knew you would think that," I said to him, "but, no, I would not have used the cliché."

Archbishop Dwyer of Birmingham used to delight in recalling how Cardinal Heenan was sometimes spoken of as 'instant wisdom'. It is true that the Cardinal did like to have things done quickly. This applied not only to his willingness to give an opinion when asked, but also to a dislike of letting things pile up when they should have been despatched without delay.

To sidetrack for a moment, I remember a plumber to whom I was giving a cup of coffee in the basement of Spanish Place Rectory, saying to me, as he looked out of the window at the church, "This is a Roman Catholic church, isn't it?" I replied in the affirmative. "Old 'Enry VIII didn't like Roman Catholics, did he?" I had to agree. "Cut their 'eads orf, didn't he?" Again, I was obliged to agree. "Didn't 'ang about, did 'e, old 'Enry?"

The reason I mention this little episode is because you could perhaps say the same of Cardinal Heenan. Not that he beheaded indiscriminately, but that 'e didn't 'ang about either!

By way of illustration, I recall how the Cardinal stood up at the end of breakfast one day and said to me, "There was an article in the *Times* last week about such-and-such: could you look it out for me? " I said, "Yes, of course," and immediately stood up. "Oh, there's no hurry" he said, as he walked out of the room. "Anytime within the next three and a half minutes," added Mgr Norris, the other occupant of the room. To the Cardinal's credit, when I related Mgr Norris's comment to him later that evening, all three of us being present, he threw back his head and laughed heartily. He was a wise man who knew his own reputation!

I do not know why it should be, but the Irish have an almost religious fervour in their appreciation of the daily newspaper. You will never find an Irishman passing by a news-stand without stopping to look at the headlines! I remember going to a hospital appointment where the young technician was Irish. I had a newspaper with me. After he had carried out his checks on my health, he said casually, "Could I just look at the headlines in your newspaper?"!

I think the best example of this level of fervour is exemplified by a visit Cardinal Heenan, then parish priest of Manor Park, made to his local school. He went into a classroom and asked the pupils what part of the catechism they were studying. The subject matter turned out to be sin – mortal and venial. "Can anyone give me an example of a mortal sin?" asked Father Heenan, looking round expectantly. A young boy shot his hand up, "Tearing the paper, Father, and it today's". Need I add that the boy was Irish? One can only imagine how he had arrived at this conclusion, but I have visions of an irate father!

About this time I had occasion to go to Cardiff, where the Ordinary was Archbishop McGrath. He was reputed to be very docile on the sanctuary. Once, when the Archbishop was conferring the sacrament of Confirmation, the (very Irish) parish priest, who was required to remove and replace the mitre on the bishop's head, discovered that the skull cap (zucchetto) kept slipping off as he put the mitre down. Twice he pushed it up under the mitre and made it stick. When it fell yet a third time - down between the Archbishop's back and the rear of the throne, he reached round, brought it to the front, presented it to the Archbishop with the request, "Would you put that little joker in your pocket?"

I related this story to Cardinal Heenan when I returned to London. Some time later, after the purification of the chalice during Mass in the Chapel of the Little Sisters of the Poor in Stoke Newington, I failed to remember to present the zucchetto on its silver salver to the Cardinal. Looking straight ahead of him, he whispered to me, "The little joker." Like him, I was facing down the chapel where there was a community of nuns and a large congregation. It was with great difficulty that I kept a straight face.

I would not like you to think that life at Archbishop's House was one long laugh. I believe we all worked hard, but we seemed to find time for humour. I think whenever your work involves a lot of different types of people you will find extraordinary characters and humorous situations.

The Vicar-General in the late 1960's was Mgr Patrick Casey, later Bishop of Brentwood. He had a great sense of humour even in the darkest days. On one occasion he and Bishop David Cashman went to visit the Carmelite Sisters who had lived in Portobello Road in London for decades. The time came when their Convent was purchased by a property developer. For all the years that they had been there, they had been treated generously by local shop-keepers who regularly donated food and goods to the Sisters. The Reverend Mother commented on this and David Cashman remarked, "How will you manage in Arkley?" (the Sisters' new home in Hertfordshire). "No one will know you there." "My Lord," said the Reverend Mother, "When God closes one door, he always opens another."

Suitably and unintentionally, rebuked, Bishop Cashman got to his feet, looked at Mgr Casey, and murmured, "Let's go to the Turf Club and have a drink!"

From that day to this, in my circle, the pious rebuke handed out to one who should have known better has been called a "Turf Club remark". There are examples too numerous to recall, but I do remember that Sister Anna Maria, my housekeeper at Spanish Place was celebrating her 80th birthday by lunching at a hotel with a group of her friends. When asked by her Superior how she intended to celebrate the occasion, instead of mentioning the lunch party, she said "Monsignor is going to say Mass for me."!

Similarly, a friend of mine jocularly asked some delightful nuns at a small nursing home whether they would celebrate the extra hour gained when the clocks were put back from BST to GMT by partying and generally having a good time. One of the nuns demurely pointed out that "Actually, we usually have a Holy Hour."

There was an occasion one Friday, when I suggested partaking of a glass of sherry before lunch. My companion looked slightly pained and said, "It's Friday. Do you think we should perhaps try and abstain?"

Each a fine example of a Turf Club remark.

CHAPTER XIX

More Secretarial Business

Among the people whose acquaintance I made at Archbishop's House was a certain Mr Tobin, the caretaker of the Cathedral Hall. Tobin was undersized, scarcely articulate and usually came into my office with the remains of a hand-rolled cigarette bobbing up and down on his lower lip. He frequently registered a complaint about some of the people who used the Hall, maltreating the stacking chairs which were used there. Sometimes he blamed the "Karachi Club" (a body who hired the Hall for their martial arts). Often they were to blame for the poor condition of the metal and fabric chairs. "It's Farver 'Arry Smiff's lot", he would say. Father Adrian Arrowsmith (as he was more accurately known) was one of the Cathedral clergy. He often made use of the Hall for a group of young people in his charge. The depredations wrought on the furniture were regularly laid upon 'Farver Arry Smiff's lot'. God rest the soul of Tobin! He had absolutely no sense of humour – I never saw him laugh. As far as he was concerned the lot of a Cathedral Hall caretaker was fraught with tribulation.

I remember meeting Tobin one morning as he was clearing up around the outside step of the Cathedral Hall. That door led out into the street, Ambrosden Avenue. He was not a happy man that day. "People are terrible," he said. "I come out 'ere this morning. Know what I found on the step? Pony and trap". I can do no more than direct you to the rhyming slang of the accomplished Cockney.

Part of my duties as Cardinal Heenan's Private Secretary was to protect him from unnecessary and unwanted intrusions on his time. Sometimes the protection became quite physical.

One evening I answered the front door bell at 9.30. A young man, slightly untidy, presented himself. I cannot remember what the nature of his request was, but I brought him in to one of the waiting rooms on the ground floor of Archbishop's House. He was slightly disturbed and I suspected that he might have been under the influence of 'unnatural substances'. We talked for a while and then he declared his intention of going to find the Cardinal. He shot out of the room made for the stairs, with me (cassocked) in hot pursuit. I managed to bring him down with a fine flying rugger tackle just before he reached the top of the stairs. He was younger than me, and despite all my efforts, he managed to reach the top and forced his way through the open door into the main part of the House. My idea was to lead him down to the little parlour at the far end of the corridor where I knew Mgr Norris would be. Between us we could eject him. As we approached the door of the chapel, he spotted the holy water stoop. He swung back suddenly and made off the way we had come. I was in pursuit at once, but he barged through the first door he came to, which led into a bedroom occupied at that time by the ninety-year old Cardinal Heard, who had arrived the previous day from Rome. Cardinal Heard woke up with a start and immediately engaged him in conversation. I was amazed. I had somehow expected the elderly man to be in a terrible state at the sudden interruption to his sleep. Realising that he was in command of the situation, I made my way swiftly down the passage to collect Mgr Norris from the parlour where he was watching the television. The Monsignor came back with me to Cardinal Heard's room and we persuaded the young man that it was time to leave the Cardinal. He came down the stairs with us quietly and left. I suspect every parish priest has similar tales to tell of opening the front door to less than desirable visitors! Certainly, as rector of Spanish Place some years later, I encountered many such characters.

I remember an advertisement for the recruitment to the Royal Navy: "Join the Navy and see the world". I didn't quite see the world, but that could almost have applied to me as Private Secretary to Cardinal Heenan, and Cardinal Hume. It was pretty much a case of wherever they went, I accompanied them. Obviously many of the trips were to Rome. We also went to France and travelled widely within the UK.

It was during my time spent as Cardinal Heenan's Secretary that he arranged for me to be 'elevated' to the lofty heights of 'Monsignor'. He felt that the title would carry more 'clout' when I had to deal with matters in his absence, while he was visiting our priests in South America. Some years later I was raised even further to the eminence of Protonotary Apostolic, courtesy of His Holiness John Paul II via Cardinal Cormac Murphy O'Connor. One of my former curates, and some of my former parishioners, have ever since addressed their letters to me with the words 'Prot. Ap.' after my name. Far from being an active notary, a prot. ap. doesn't have to do anything particularly. He just rejoices in the title and is cheered to see it appended to his name on an envelope. It is essentially the highest grade of Monsignor and an honorary title, and I am delighted to have it.

Another title I seemed to acquire at around this time was that of 'Fierce Fred'. I am told that when I was Cardinal Heenan's secretary I was often referred to in this way by the clergy of Westminster Cathedral. I don't know why, but I can only guess that I gained this soubriquet because of my eagerness to protect the Cardinal from unwanted intrusions on his time, such as that which I described earlier. The name must have been whispered quietly in those hallowed corridors; because I did not find out about it until after I had retired, when my former Director of Music at Spanish Place, Dr Terry Worroll, inadvertently let it slip.

CHAPTER XX

More Sport – Tennis

I made several new friends while I was with the Cardinal. One day when the Cardinal had to go to the studios of ITN to record an interview, I, of course, was required to accompany him. Whilst he was doing his interview I waited in the Green Room. Suddenly the door opened and in came a man whom I recognised as Reginald Bosanquet, the newsreader. "Do you mind if I put the television on?" he asked. "There's a match on at Wimbledon I would like to see." I agreed readily, telling him that I, too, liked tennis. And we watched the match together. It transpired that Reggie played twice a week (including Christmas Day!) all year round. He asked me if I would like to join the group with whom he played. This was the first opportunity I had had to play tennis since I had left St Edmund's in 1966, so I was delighted to accept his invitation. Thus started my long association with a group that played twice weekly on a private court in York House Terrace, Kensington.

The personnel in the group changed over the years. Among the members were, Ivor Mills (newsreader), Rory McPherson (newsreader), Iain Johnson (who worked for the BBC), Roderic Bullough (businessman), (Jenny Hopkirk (the wife of the rally driver, Paddy Hopkirk), Colin Thubron (the highly acclaimed travel writer), Celia Buckley (who was a J.P.), Micky Bowen (who was Archbishop of Southwark), and – as I have already said – Reggie, and myself. Annie Bridges was another invaluable member of our little band. She was Reggie's secretary at ITN, and it was she who had the vital job of rounding us all up regularly for our games and lunches.

Whenever we played together we always went for lunch to a wine bar in Kensington High Street, run by Jimmy James. Jimmy – I am sure he wouldn't mind my saying – was an enthusiast whose over-enthusiasm didn't quite match his aptitude for the game. Later he moved to the Isle of Man, and, sadly, we lost touch.

We played regularly and greatly enjoyed each other's company – as well as keeping fit, of course. One thing that sticks in my mind was when a ball was hit out of the court over a wall at the far end. Rory and Reggie were playing together at that end, and Reggie climbed over the wall to retrieve the ball. It seemed to take him a long time; and eventually Rory looked over the wall to see where he was. In fact, Reggie was lying face-down on the ground with blood trickling from the corner of his mouth. We approached him and turned him over, and soon he began to recover. Rory wanted to fetch an ambulance, but Reggie wouldn't hear of it. Now I knew that Reggie was subject to epileptic fits; but I had never witnessed one before this. I assumed that the blood came from a cut lip or tongue. Reggie insisted that he was perfectly alright and that we should all go and have lunch together as usual.

When I was relating this story at supper that evening in Archbishop's House, with the Cardinal and John Crowley (now Bishop of Middlesborough), the latter excused himself and left the table. Later he explained to me that he had a 'thing' about blood and my graphic account of Reggie with blood oozing from his mouth proved too much for him. It seems that some hematophobics cannot even stand the mention of the b-word without turning a little green around the gills.

We (the tennis players) were a lively bunch and the conversation around the lunch table was always animated and sprinkled with enthusiastic debate. On many occasions I had to fight my Catholic corner, but the arguments were always good-humoured.

Reggie became unwell in the early eighties. It is no secret that he did like a drink or two and this is what led to his pancreatitis. I called on him in his flat in the King's Road. "Freddie," he said, "I am finished." He knew that his illness was so advanced that there was no cure. We sat and talked for a long time: I was very fond of Reggie and I knew I would miss him.

Sadly, but as we had expected, Reggie died. He was only in his early fifties. I officiated at his cremation and later, his daughter and his common-law wife took part in a little ceremony in the garden at Spanish Place. There we buried the little urn containing Reggie's ashes. At the cremation ceremony I spoke briefly and so did Andrew Gardner (principal ITN newsreader). I recorded how Reggie and I used to argue about religious matters. I didn't see why he should expect the Catholic Church to endorse his sexual morals: he, for his part, simply regarded the Church as the long-stop of the Mafia! Andrew spoke warmly of Reggie, calling him a "one-off". And so he was.

The relationship I had with the tennis players continues to this very day. We meet regularly, although – since having a stroke in the eighties – I was no longer able to join them on the courts. Despite that, the happy group continues to invite me to join them for lunch whenever they meet.

CHAPTER XXI

Some Sadness

In total I worked with Cardinal Heenan for almost ten years. They were very happy and fruitful years from my point of view. I had always admired the Cardinal. He was highly respected both within and without the Church. I suppose it is true to say that he was the chief spokesman on religious affairs in the country – just as his successor – Basil Hume was to become later. He had a confident and fluent manner when dealing with the media, and was good at delivering what has become known as the 'sound-bite' – the apposite comment, which could often form a headline. He was on easy terms with Archbishop Michael Ramsay of Canterbury, and indeed invited him to preach in the Cathedral. Later that evening, after the Cardinal had gone to bed, I was sitting with Archbishop Ramsay watching the television news. Included in the news was an excerpt from Ramsay's sermon of that evening. He was shown doing a particularly Ramsayian thing – the well-balanced phrase. The words quoted were, "and, sometimes, we upset one another by the things we say and the things we do." We sat there and chuckled at that balanced phrase!

I always felt that I had a good friend in Cardinal Heenan. We both hailed from the same diocese (Brentwood), but as the Cardinal would sometimes remind me when he thought I was getting above myself, "Remember, Fred, Bishop Doubleday accepted me; but he turned you down!" This was true, but then, in my own defence, I could say that Bishop Doubleday turned most people down! He was always afraid that the diocese would be short of money and he could not afford to support a student for the priesthood. He used to import his priests 'ready-made' from Ireland. It was cheaper, and at that time, there were plenty of them. Eventually my parish priest applied to Cardinal Hinsley to have me accepted for Westminster and the rest, as they say, is some of the history I have already covered.

It was not very long after I started working with the Cardinal, in 1966, that he returned from a visit to his brother-in-law, Sydney Reynolds. Sydney had been suffering from shingles and the Cardinal picked up the herpes virus in his spinal fluid. This led to a condition known as encephalitis – an inflammation of the lining of the brain. He suffered quite severe headaches, as a result, and the virus took some time to work itself out. I do not think he ever again had the stamina and energy which had marked his activities before this time, but even a disabled Cardinal Heenan was a good deal more able than the average man!

In 1974 I went to Scotland with my sister, Patricia, for a holiday. While we were in Barra, in the Outer Hebrides, I had a telephone call from Mgr Norris to say that the Cardinal was ill. I made the decision to return to London immediately – abandoning Pat in Benbecula to be entertained and accommodated by the local parish priest, Fr Calum McClellan.

On my arrival back in London I found the Cardinal confined to bed. I called his doctor, who diagnosed diabetes, and the Cardinal accepted our advice that he should go into hospital for blood cleansing treatment, the blood sugar level being excessively high. He was reluctant to go as he was due to chair a meeting of the Hierarchy the following week. He eventually agreed to my driving him to Westminster Hospital where he was admitted for the necessary treatment. In the event it was all too late. He died from renal failure, about four days later in Westminster Hospital. It was 8th October 1975.

84 My next task, of course, was to set about arranging his funeral

Mass and burial. I had always known that the Cardinal wished to be buried – not in the crypt like his predecessors – but in the body of the Cathedral where people would see his tomb and remember more readily to pray for the repose of his soul. He wanted to be buried near the Twelfth Station of the Cross. As it was not normally permitted to bury people under the floor of a comparatively recently constructed building, I had to get permission from the Authorities. Not wanting to waste time, I telephoned Downing Street and spoke to the Prime Minister's Secretary. Later, PM Harold Wilson spoke to me on the telephone and assured me that I could go ahead; "If there is any objection raised to this I shall have an order made in council which will be retrospective and endorse all that we have agreed to." I then set up a small body of priests to co-ordinate arrangements for the funeral and see to the accommodation of visiting clerics from mainland Europe.

The Requiem Mass took place in a packed Westminster Cathedral just one week after Cardinal Heenan's death. There was an influx of prelates from Europe and the UK. The service was broadcast on the radio and television, and I can remember realising a moment or two before the event, that I was supposed to be delivering one of the readings. I had been so busy that I had not prepared it in any way. As it turned out, it did not matter – somehow I managed on what you might call auto-pilot.

So it was that Cardinal John Carmel Heenan was laid to rest. May Almighty God have mercy on his soul. He was a great man and a fine friend and I knew I would miss him.

What I have omitted to say was that, two days before the Cardinal's death, my own beloved mother had died, at the age of 84. She had been living at home in the care of my dear younger sister, Pat, but – as she became more and more frail – I arranged for her to go into a hospital run by Daughters of Charity, at Eastcote in Middlesex. Full credit must go to Pat for her many years of care, but it had become increasingly difficult for her to continue to look after Mother and hold down a full-time job at the Admiralty Research Laboratory. Both Pat and I were at our mother's bedside when she died. So it was that I was faced with the great sadness of losing – within the space of a week – two people who were very close and important to me. May they both rest in peace.

CHAPTER XXII

Cardinal Basil Hume

One of the Auxiliary Bishops of Westminster at this time was the Right Reverend Christopher Butler, OSB, the former Abbot of Downside Abbey. During the interregnum following the death of Cardinal Heenan, Bishop Butler came up to live in Archbishop's House. Normally he lived down in Hertfordshire, the area of which he was bishop. He lived in Archbishop's House for about four months, while the new archbishop of Westminster was being selected. He was a wonderful companion with a lively sense of humour. During this time I got to know him very well, and I understand that he was quite happy to bask in the peace and quiet he received as a result of my Fierce Fred Rotweiller act!

Some time later I opened the front door of Archbishop's House to admit Cardinal Basil Hume, fresh from Ampleforth Abbey. He tells the story that he rang the doorbell of Archbishop's House, was mistaken for a vagrant and sent to Clergy House to ask for some food. A good story – but not as I remember it happening! In fact, I opened the door myself to admit Basil Hume to Archbishop's House. As we went up the red-carpeted staircase, I said to him, "I have now been here for 10 years: I shall stay for as long or short a time as you wish." I showed him to the Archbishop's study and bedroom and left him to settle in.

It wasn't long before Basil decided that he would take a room on the top floor where he could – paradoxically – "lie low" (a favourite expression of his) when he wanted to. It is fair to say that Basil was initially a 'reluctant' Archbishop of Westminster. He loved his time at Ampleforth and was devoted to the community there. He was born in that part of Newcastle called Jesmond, and his mother and family lived in that same area. His attachment to the north of England was considerable and was shown in the book he wrote about the northern saints.

In the event, Basil Hume proved to be a very popular cardinal. Even Her Majesty the Queen referred to him as "my Cardinal". I remember Bishop Casey telling me about an Irish parish priest whom he visited on a trip to Ireland when he was seeking students for the priesthood. "Tell me, my Lord," said the priest, "how it is that the English are making such a fuss about the new Archbishop of Westminster." "Well," said Casey, "I don't know really. He was the abbot of Ampleforth – which was quite a distinction; he was very much an English aristocrat, of course, with a French mother and a heart physician for a father. His father wasn't a Catholic."

"Ah – that's it," said the Irish priest, "He had a bit of the Protestant in him, and the English love that!"

Despite his reluctance, in the course of time he settled into the job remarkably well. His later interviews with the media showed a steady advance in dealing with this kind of encounter, which he had initially found difficult, being quite hesitant and reserved by nature. By contrast, his predecessor, Cardinal Heenan, had always been extremely fluent and assured when dealing with the media. When he was a parish priest in Manor Park (east London) he had been known as 'The Radio Priest', so frequent were his appearances on the radio. However, as time went on, Basil Hume acquired greater assurance and confidence in dealing with the Press. The impression I got was that the media were well-disposed towards him and, apart from one difficult interview with Ludovic Kennedy, he was always given a fairly easy passage.

In all truth, I never really felt the same rapport with Basil Hume as I had with his predecessor. This was probably due to a certain reserve in his manner. He was more of a contemplative than John Heenan, which is not to say that Cardinal Heenan was lacking in any way in his prayer life; it was just that he didn't have the monastic stamp of Cardinal Hume. That being said, Basil Hume and I got on well together and enjoyed an easy relationship and had plenty of laughs together.

Once when we were flying back from Paris, we were diverted from Heathrow because of fog. We landed in Manchester and were given railway tickets and food vouchers for the journey back to London. We set off and soon went along to the Buffet Car to collect our rations. I suggested that the Cardinal wait in the compartment while I would see to the food. There was, as you might imagine, quite a queue in the buffet car and one solitary steward was doing his best to make sandwiches for all the extra passengers from the aeroplane. Near me there stood an indignant Frenchman who proclaimed his nationality by being irritated at having to queue. We English are quite accustomed to this, of course. He complained to the overworked steward, *"Qui est le responsable?"* and when the poor man went on solidly with his work, the Frenchman threw his hands up and uttered the unprintable-in-English curse, *"Merde!"* "Mad, am I?" said the clearly uncomprehending steward. "I reckon he's the mad one," came his phlegmatic reply. I related all this when I eventually got back to the compartment with our rations, and Cardinal Hume greatly enjoyed the anecdote.

Basil Hume was a very patient man but even he sometimes gave way to exasperation. There was one occasion when he was required to go to the Dorchester Hotel for a Reception given by Archbishop Athenagorus, who was the Greek Orthodox archbishop of Thyateira. He duly turned up at the hotel, in zucchetto (red skull cap) and piped cassock with red buttons, dismissed the driver and entered the hotel. A waiter approached, enquiring if he could be of some help. When the Cardinal explained his reason for being there, the waiter said, "That Reception has been cancelled, sir; didn't they let you know?" Clearly, 'they' hadn't. This landed the Cardinal on the pavement in Park Lane, in full canonicals, but without a penny in his pocket.

Meanwhile, back at the ranch, I was entertaining the ITN newsreader, Reginald Bosanquet, one of my tennis chums whom I mentioned earlier. We were enjoying a pre-supper drink. "Gin and tonic?" said I. "Yes" came the reply, "but don't worry too much about the tonic." Suddenly we heard a shout from the stairs. It was Basil Hume returning prematurely from the Dorchester, asking if anyone had a quid for the taxi. Reggie stumped up, and the Cardinal stumped in. He threw his zucchetto onto the table, declaring, "That's the end of Ecumenism!" A risky remark in view of the presence of a journalist! Reggie may have related the story privately, but he never read it out on the News at Ten.

You can just imagine it: *Bong!* "Cardinal announces the end of Ecumenical movement."

Incidentally, writing the word 'ecumenical' reminds me of a parishioner in Redhill, where Professor Jack Scarisbrick was on the Ecumenical Commission. The word always caused this particular man trouble. Eventually he settled for "The Unichemical Movement"! Close enough!

Cardinal Heenan wrote two volumes of autobiography and a book on the priesthood. Cardinal Hume wrote several books, some of which were compilations of his various addresses, sermons, etc. These had been carefully recorded and put together by Heather Craufurd, a woman I was later to meet as a fellow-resident at St Peter's in Vauxhall. Heather was devoted to Basil Hume; he could certainly do no wrong in her eyes and I think that was a view which was very commonly held.

As it turned out, I worked with Basil Hume for about two years. He knew that I had already spent the previous ten years at Archbishop's House, and he felt that I would benefit from experiencing life as a parish priest. When Monsignor George Tomlinson retired from St James's, Spanish Place, in central London, the Cardinal appointed me as his successor. In the past, I had sometimes been reluctant, or disappointed – initially at any rate – to be moved from what I was doing; but this time I was happy to accept the new challenge. In a sense, being a parish priest was what I had been waiting for since being ordained in 1950. The year now was 1977.

CHAPTER XXIII

Spanish Place

I should perhaps, first of all, explain why the church was known – by Catholics from London and further a-field – as 'Spanish Place', despite the fact that it is located between George Street and Blandford Street, in Marylebone. The road opposite the church is called Spanish Place. The reason that this name was given to the parish was that, in the latter part of the 18th century, an Italianate church stood in Spanish Place and was the chapel of the Spanish Embassy. The building, which now houses the Wallace Collection, is called Hertford House and it was originally the residence of the Spanish Ambassador. When the Embassy moved to Belgrave Square, the chapel was demolished by the owner of the land on which it stood; flats were built in its place. The parishioners began to collect money to build a new church, and when they had collected £30,000, the site of the present church became available and they bought it. This was towards the end of the 19th century. King Alphonso XIII of Spain helped them to acquire the site and the church was opened in 1890. Strangely it remained unconsecrated until the year 1947 – which is the time when I first became acquainted with that church. I was a member of a *schola cantorum*, which went up from St Edmund's College to sing all the Latin chants contained in the Rite of Consecration. The recently ordained Charlie McGowan – mentioned earlier in these reminiscences – was curate there, and the rector was Bishop George Craven.

So, thirty years later, I was to return to Spanish Place as Rector. Why Rector? There are about five parishes in the Westminster

Diocese which have a Rector rather than a parish priest, and a rectory rather than a presbytery. These parishes had been formed before the Restoration of the Hierarchy (in 1850) and were known as 'Missions', and the priests in charge were called 'Rectors'. And the tradition has remained.

The years at Spanish Place turned out to be the happiest and most rewarding time of my life as a priest. Once again, I was surprised at how happy I was. My time with the Cardinals had been very enjoyable and rewarding, but I accepted the new appointment with enthusiasm and just a little trepidation. I had never been in charge of a parish and St James's is a very large and important parish in the diocese with a fluctuating congregation. There was, what you might call, a hard core of resident parishioners – many of whom had lived in the Marylebone area for a good deal of time; but there were also many visitors, and people who worked in the area often came to the lunchtime Mass there.

In the beginning, I had two curates – Father Jeremy Davies and Father Peter Keenan. Very different in character and temperament, they were admirable curates – hard-working and loyal. It seemed too good to be true. Sadly, Peter became unwell and suffered deeply from depression and I had to recommend to Cardinal Hume that he be transferred to another parish.

Jeremy stayed with me for a total of sixteen years. I had various other curates in that time: a Pole, an American, and a Legionary of Christ who hailed from Limerick. This last was Fr Donal Corrie, a wonderful, twinkly-eyed, immensely devout priest. He endeared himself to me by being a fan of every type of sport. I even caught him one afternoon watching cricket on the television – and he an Irishman!

About this time I devised all manner of daft games to brighten up the dish-washing periods after meals. One of these games involved the lobbing of a cork (from the occasional bottle of wine!!) into a small plastic pot which resided on the draining board of the sink – a 'sink-tidy', I believe it is called. Another game consisted of hurling the knotted-up (necessary for aerodynamics) tea-towel into the open door of the front-loading washing machine. Donal proved himself to be adept at all these forms of sport! He had a peculiar habit of sending the cork on a flight path with a graceful over-arm motion and a good follow-through. He later returned to Rome to work for Cardinal Ratzinger, who subsequently became Pope Benedict XVI. I wonder whether he ever told the Pope-in-waiting of his sporting prowess in the kitchens of Spanish Place! Somehow I doubt it!

Another of my curates was Fr Christopher Gawecki, a Polish priest with a rather fiery temperament but also a great sense of loyalty to me. After one of his visits to the land of his fathers he arrived back with a bottle of Rectified Polish Spirit, which was about 98% proof. This was proudly produced for us to sample at dinner one evening. Part-way through the sampling, Christopher was called away from the table to take a telephone call. While he was absent I emptied the contents of the bottle into a jug and then filled the bottle with water. When he returned to the room it was to find me pouring the contents of this bottle (water) down the drain in the sink, while proclaiming, "We can't possibly drink this – it's ghastly." He was horrified – until we eventually owned up to the truth.

At this point I feel I should mention Sister Anna-Maria. When I went to Spanish Place, the household was being managed by Sister Anna-Maria and Sister Gottharda. Sister Anna-Maria was 70 years of age. She was a small, wiry, hard-working Pallottine nun from East Prussia. She ran the household like clockwork. Her capacity for work seemed inexhaustible. I mentioned just now the dish-washing undertaken by the priests – I should add that Sister Anna-Maria was at the time in the scullery scrubbing the pots. Her meals were legendary. She operated on the principle that if she provided enough different vegetable dishes at meal-times, everybody would find something they liked. This resulted in wonderful meals – and terrific soups the following day! I had a fondness for cheese soufflé for supper – and she regularly prepared these for me – although I never got her to admit how many eggs were included in her recipe! Lunches were quite often almost 'open-house'. She was never fazed by the number of people I invited. I have to admit that I am quite a gregarious chap, who loves the company of other people. I used to dispense *Venerabile* (English College in Rome) 'Hooch' (a not very secret recipe!) in my sitting-room to my guests before meals. I also remember offering liqueurs to some friends after dinner on one occasion. "There's some Crème de Menthe in here," I said from the depths of my drinks cabinet. One chap accepted the offer with alacrity. However, when I came to pour out some of the contents of the bottle, it fell out with a couple of clunks into the glass. "I think that might be past its best," I said. I had never bought any Crème de Menthe, so I obviously inherited it from a previous rector – who knows which – and it had been around for so long that it had solidified!

While Sister Anna-Maria's cooking and household management were exemplary, some of her nursing methods could tend towards the dramatic. There was an occasion when I developed a nasty dose of 'flu and could do no more than stay weakly in my bed. Eventually, feeling hot and sticky from my heightened temperature, I got up and expressed the desire for a bath. "Death!" shrieked Sister A-M at me, sure that this would be the certain outcome of such an outrageous course of action. You would think I had suggested a swim in the Thames! I meekly headed back to bed and more ministrations from Sister A-M. Her care for 'her' priests was non-pareil. She is a truly great nun, who finally left Spanish Place when she was into her nineties and after I had retired to Vauxhall. She returned to her convent in Macclesfield, where she continues to care for the other sisters there – most, if not all, of them younger than her, such is her fortitude.

CHAPTER XXIV

Curates – and Vagrants

I was blessed to be surrounded at Spanish Place, by wonderful people. Fr Andrew Wadsworth was another of my curates who is certainly worthy of mention. Andrew is an extremely intelligent, energetic and enthusiastic priest, who has a great sense of humour, not to mention a wonderful singing voice. He performed as one of the Three Tenors in the clergy Revue on at least one occasion. He was also regularly called upon to sing the *Exultet* on Holy Saturday, just before Easter. There was one occasion when he was required to sing this lengthy piece twice in one evening – first at Harrow School and then in St James's; he managed perfectly.

I know Andrew would not mind me saying that he is a well-covered man. He did attempt a diet once (to my knowledge) when Sister Anna–Maria was instructed to provide him with a slimming spread for his breakfast toast. He took one bite of the toast and remarked, "This is terrible; anyone got any butter?" And that was the end of dieting for Andrew. I am happy to say that he continues to thrive and work extremely hard. Andrew was with me for about five years before being appointed Catholic chaplain to the boys at Harrow School – a job for which he is admirably suited. We still keep in touch and Andrew's solicitude for my well-being is wonderful. Whenever we have occasion to concelebrate at Mass, he is always there at my side offering a strong arm for me to lean on as I teeter (as an octogenarian tends to) up and down steps.

I mentioned, some time back, that I had a stroke. It happened one morning at breakfast while I was Rector at Spanish Place. The telephone rang and I went to the office to answer it. It was Bishop Brewer of Shrewsbury. In the course of our conversation he mentioned several facts which I thought I should note down. I had some difficulty in picking up a pencil and even more difficulty in using it. Despite not being a medical man ("I never really bothered!" c.f. Tony Hancock) I realised straightaway that I was having a stroke. As soon as the telephone conversation finished, I buzzed my curate – Jeremy Davies – who had qualified as a doctor, before being ordained. He came downstairs and I asked him if I looked 'normal' (I thought my mouth might have sagged a bit.) He reassured me that I looked fine, as I put forward my diagnosis. He helped me upstairs to my bedroom.

I knew of a consultant neurologist living in Marylebone – Dr Reginald Kelly. My curate telephoned him and asked that he come and see me. He thought it would be a good idea to rest in bed until I felt more comfortable. At lunchtime I went down and began to serve the soup, and realised that I had barely the strength to lift the ladle – I returned to bed! Reg Kelly thought I should go into hospital and telephoned the Matron at the King Edward VII hospital. She took me in at once and I spent three weeks in that wonderful hospital, being thoroughly spoilt. I was very lucky; the stroke left me with no more than a slightly heavy right leg and right arm. Nothing else was affected, thanks be to God.

Father Jeremy Davies was completely different in character from Andrew, but equally hard-working. He was a quiet, serious and conscientious man who spent a good deal of time in prayer and reading. He also came out with the odd unexpected fact. He told me once, in all seriousness: "Do you know – that the word 'entrails' occurs only once in the New Testament?" I had to confess that I didn't – and I have searched ever since for an occasion to bring this fact to public notice! Which brings me on to sermons.

You may remember the story of my tutorial with Dr Plumb in Cambridge, when I presented myself to him fresh (I used the word advisedly) from the rugger pitch, complete with muddy knees – but incomplete essay. Well, I can report that – in this respect – I had not made much improvement. I am – to this day – a last minute man – something of a brinkman, you might say. I could often be found flying down the stairs at Spanish Place – heading for the 10.30am Sunday Mass, clutching an incomplete sermon and composing the last lines in my head. My sermons on paper were something to behold – with arrows to indicate transposing sentences, extra boxes on the reverse of the pages, lines written up the sides and asterisks a go-go. But somehow I seemed to manage to deliver the homilies without too much trouble. I can't say they received standing ovations, but I didn't have too many complaints!

One Sunday, in mid-sermon a well-known local – somewhat the worse for drink – staggered up the aisle. I had been preaching on the supremacy of Peter and was just quoting "What so ever thou shalt bind upon earth ..." when the drunk joined in – rather impressively, it has to be said – "... shall be considered bound in heaven," he roared. He was helped out after his enthusiastic contribution.

I recall another occasion when a drunk appeared in the church and started making a nuisance of himself. Another gentleman of the road, who originated in Northern Ireland, sprang into action and began to hustle him out of the church. As he passed me he said, "Will I affect a citizen's arrest here?" "No, thank you" I said, "Just take him out." This helpful individual was often to be found sitting in the doorway of a bank in the High Street begging for spare change and announcing "We accept cheques." He was a rather superior beggar.

As rector of a church in the centre of London, I was treated to many encounters with heavy drinkers and beggars. They used to ring the doorbell of the rectory and ask for money for 'a cup of tea'. I made the policy of not giving them money but offering to get them hot food, if they were hungry. We also kept a supply of small packets of biscuits to hand out to these rather disappointed characters. One such gentleman turned down the offer of food, and stuck to his request for money. "Look," I said, "I don't feel under any obligation to finance your drinking." He pulled himself up to his full height and said rather indignantly, "I don't drink ... I gamble." I was so disarmed by this honesty, that he got a couple of quid from me.

Vastly less endearing characters were those who tried to steal money from the candle boxes in the church. They developed a *modus operandi* involving wire and chewing gum. (I knew that this was the method employed because the local constabulary printed a news-letter on one occasion, warning the local churches to be on their guard against such larceny – and describing in much fuller detail than I have done, exactly how the successful thief managed to net his illegal gain. I remember thinking how very helpful that was for anyone who hadn't worked out how to do it!)

One chap who had worked out how to do it was busy about his thieving business while, unbeknownst to him, a workman was occupied in the choir-loft on some repair work to the organ. When this workman had finished he came to me and asked, "Do you ever 'ave money nicked from them collecting boxes in the church?" I said that I suspected I did. He then went on, "I saw someone messin' about with that box near the statue, so I shouted down, ''ere, what the b....y 'ell d'ya think you're doin'?' He looked round and couldn't see nobody. I reckon 'e thought it was Almighty God shoutin' at 'im!"

On one occasion, a parishioner of mine heard the tell-tale sound of someone rifling a candle box. She kept turning around and glaring at this thief to try and shame him into stopping. Eventually, he called out loudly, "Stop turning around. No wonder your prayers aren't answered!" Just what this world needs: a thieving theologian!

CHAPTER XXV

The Church – and Shooting Gallery

I was delighted to come across a long-standing tradition when I arrived at Spanish Place. It was the singing of the National Anthem at the end of the 10.30am sung Mass. The tradition dated back to a Sunday in 1940 when the organist, Mr Hasbury, seeing parishioners coming to the church, pale-faced and low of spirit after a night of German bombing, decided at the end of the Mass to play the National Anthem. People joined in heartily. Afterwards, the Rector, Monsignor Tynan, told the organist, "That was an excellent idea, Mr Hasbury; let's have it every Sunday." This continued until my successor at Spanish Place (in 1998) decided to end the tradition, for reasons best known to himself.

The choir at Spanish Place – usually consisting of about nine singers – was extremely good. This was due, not only to the quality of the voices, but also to the great musical direction of Dr Terry Worroll and his assistant, Jerry Pieti. Both of these wonderful gentlemen gave of their time and efforts unstintingly in the service of the music at the church. Life was always busy somehow in the Rectory. Indeed, Terry used to complain that he could never catch me in my office; he recalls that most of my decisions with regard to the music and the organ were made on the staircase – both going up and going down!

It was a wonderfully happy time. The Rectory was always busy and, as I have already said, run smoothly by Sister Anna-Maria, my housekeeper. Patricia and her sister, Thelma, looked after things in the office, while Dan Branley ran the Sacristy. When he retired, he was succeeded in that position by Christoper Daly – who is very keen on having lots of servers, acolytes, incense and candles.

Speaking of candles reminds me of the story of a Filipina girl who came to me with her non-Catholic, English fiancé. They were to be married. I decided to question the girl about her religious practice – Mass attendance, reception of the sacraments, etc. After a while, the fiancé, (a Londoner) intervened – feeling, I suppose that I was giving her a hard time. "Y' know, Farver. I've bin in the Philippines, and it's not quite the same aht there. It's mostly *stetues* and *kendals*." Which reminds me, I wonder if you have noticed that whenever a television or film production company wishes to suggest that a church in which they are filming is Catholic, they always set the place ablaze with flickering candles. I know we like our 'statues and candles' – but they are not exactly the centre of our worship.

The maintenance of the church itself was of primary importance to me. Sir John Paul Getty II was a great benefactor of Spanish Place. He paid for the cleaning of the church, inside and out, the repair of the roof, and the re-gilding of the Sanctuary and of the chapels of the Sacred Heart and Our Blessed Lady.

I came to know Paul when he was a patient in the London Clinic, where I was chaplain. After his time in hospital he was confined to barracks in his flat near Pall Mall. I went there often to bring him Holy Communion and we became good friends. We shared a great interest in cricket and Paul built a beautiful cricket ground on his estate near Wormsley. It really was a superb ground, nestling in the smooth hills of the Oxfordshire countryside. There was a thatched pavilion on one side of the ground and a similarly thatched scoring box on the other. It was all idyllic – and still is, as Paul's widow, Victoria, continues to hold matches at the ground in memory of her husband. She entertains many of her late husband's friends in generous style. Paul loved cricket and cricketing people and I have to say I have had much the same experience. Paul was introduced to cricket by – of all people – the pop singer Mick Jagger, whom I met with his father, in Paul's box at Lord's Cricket Ground. Paul's philanthropy is legendary and I was delighted to be able to leave the church in excellent condition – largely as a result of Paul's benefactions – when I retired. I feel I should add here that I never, ever went to Paul with my begging bowl. His interest in St James's was genuine and his generosity was spontaneous. On a number of occasions I was asked to recommend to Paul various worthy causes. I always declined to do so, on the grounds that I never asked Paul for a penny; it would have been an abuse of my friendship with him to do so.

At least we never had to have any of the stained glass replaced. I mention this because, from time to time, pigeons trespassed within the church. They were a great nuisance, flying from one end of the great church to the other and scattering droppings as well as the dust from the sills high above the Sanctuary. At first I tried to trap them with the approved method of food and garden sieve. But they were too wily for this to work. Eventually there was nothing for it: they had to be shot (see front cover!). I took a powerful air-gun into the church and positioned myself in the choir gallery, up in the *triforium*. When the pigeons settled – well away from any stained glass – I potted them with the gun, fitted with a telescopic sight. I managed to bag a brace. I know they are all God's creatures, but after all, Our Lord did throw the money-lenders out of the temple and overturned their tables and these pigeons were at least as much to be deplored! At any event, it was comforting to know that I was still possessed of the 'physical fitness, determination and nerve control' required by marksmen in my Officer Training Corps days.

When I retired many years later, I was unable to take all of my possessions to my small retirement flat. It was with no small degree of surprise and shock that my successor said to one of my ex-parishioners, "There's a rifle in Monsignor Miles's wardrobe!" "Yes," she replied calmly. "It was for use when parishioners upset him badly." He believed her for almost a full second.

CHAPTER XXVI

The Box

Shortly after I arrived at Spanish Place the priests at Opus Dei offered to hear confessions in the church daily. It was a great advantage in a central London church like St James's to be able to offer confessions every weekday at lunchtime. I got to know most of the priests of Opus Dei because whoever was on confessional duty used to stay for lunch with us in the Rectory.

I, of course, took many a turn in 'The Box'. Without breaking the seal of the confessional, I can tell you about one penitent who crashed down on the kneeler and said, "I've been livin' riochus, Farver", from which I understood him to have been living something of a riotous life.

There was an occasion when a small girl came into the Box to make her confession. I concluded with the words, "Go in peace, and say a prayer for me." I looked up and there she still was – her eyes just above the ledge, staring fixedly at me. I repeated my advice and still the eyes were fixed upon me. "It's time now to go and say your penance in the church," I suggested. The eyes – and the rest of the girl – remained unmoved. Short of telling her that she would find girls her own age outside, I tried every way to shift her. At last, in exasperation, I said "Go away!" And finally she fled!

Confession, or the sacrament of reconciliation as it is now known, is practised less these days than in the past. However, the numbers of people who go to Confession at Westminster

Cathedral never seem to tail off. There have been a number of occasions when I have sat in a queue at the Cathedral, waiting for almost an hour to make my confession. At least twice, I got up out of the queue, went to the sacristy, collected my name-plate and a stole and positioned myself in the second Box – to help shorten the queue and speed things up a bit. The priests at the Cathedral must have found the queues frustrating too, as I was once asked – for my penance – to hear the confession of the confessor to whom I had just confessed!

I was Provost of the Cathedral Chapter for about fifteen years. We held meetings monthly, and sometimes I would go and do a stint – if I may call it that – hearing confessions after the meetings. I would go down into the church in my purple cassock; I am sure that this acted as something of a deterrent, as people thought I looked 'official' and fearsome and was likely to hand out hefty penances.

Another deterrent to making confession is to discover that the priest in the box is someone you know quite well. Cardinal Hume was hearing confessions once in Lourdes, when his typist approached the box. She saw it was the Cardinal and turned away saying, "Oh – I'm not going to you!"

However, it would seem that not everyone minds confessing to a priest of their close acquaintance. One Saturday evening I was leaving the church in Farm Street when an elderly gentleman enquired of the priest at the door, "Is Father Devas here?" "He's in the house," said the young priest. "Will you tell him: Major Hawkins; fortnight; the usual things – I'll say the usual penance." (N.B. the name has been changed to protect the innocent – or should that be 'the guilty'?)

As I got older, my hearing began to get a little deficient. There was one lady who came to confess and seemed a little hesitant. When I asked if there was a problem, she replied, "Well you see Father, I'm a bit mutt'n." "What do you mean?" I asked.

"Mutt an' Jeff – deaf" she explained, helpfully. It was the first time I had experienced the use of Cockney rhyming slang in the confessional – the first and only time. My reply was, "I'm a bit mutt'n, too – so shall we both speak up a bit?"

When I retired to Vauxhall the priest who used to live in the room next-door was an absolute delight of a fellow called Fr Denis Ryan – God rest him. He had been seriously deaf most of his life and told the story of a regular penitent who, I am sure, must have been Irish. He knew Fr Ryan well and was aware of his deafness. No sooner had he entered the box than he started to shout out to the good Father Ryan his racing tip of the day: "Billy Boy, 3.30, Kempton;." before settling down to make his confession. I can only imagine the frenzied scribbling and note-taking going on outside the box as everyone tried to take advantage of the loudly offered tip!

CHAPTER XXVII

Medical Matters

I have already touched on my medical history when I wrote about my stroke. Some time after that I needed a hip replacement. For this I went to Dublin because I had been introduced to a surgeon, James Sheehan, who operated at the Black Rock Clinic. All this was organised for me by a delightful Holy Ghost father at Black Rock College – Fr O'Malley, God rest his soul. The Clinic was immaculately clean and great pains were taken to ensure that there were no infections among the patients. To this end I was required – in preparation for the surgery – to have a series of iodine baths: about four in two days. By then I was pretty squeaky clean and ready to face the knife. The operation went very well, thank God and thanks to James Sheehan. One day, instead of my usual nurse, there came a Northern Ireland girl, who announced to me in a broad Ulster accent something that sounded like: "I'll be with you in a few minutes to take your blood pressure and check your wind." I could not imagine what form the latter procedure would take, but I was pretty apprehensive. I needn't have worried. What she had pronounced as "wind", was, in fact, "wound", and it was this she was coming to check. That was a relief, I can tell you.

I had expected that, once I had recovered from the surgery, I would be able to leap on my bike (my preferred method of getting about in central London). As it turned out, I was on crutches for about thirteen weeks. Mr Sheehan had insisted that I used the crutches for as long as that. The result was that, when I put them aside, I had no tendency to limp.

My only other major surgery was in 2003 when I had to have an aneurysm removed from my right leg. It is a long and complicated story which I need not relate in detail. Suffice to say that it involved contracting MRSA, the 'superbug', at St Thomas's Hospital, and being cured of it at the King Edward VII Hospital. I shall be for ever grateful for the great generosity shown me by several good friends who donated to the expense of being treated in such a fine private hospital. At this time I also had a pacemaker fitted, as my heartbeat was apparently in need of help to keep it regular. I think that is all there is to say about my health – I don't want to become a valetudinarian! By and large I am not too bad at accepting the things that life throws at me. Life really is too short to fight against its tribulations: that seems to me to be the healthiest attitude to try and have.

CHAPTER XXVIII

The Kindness of Folk

While I was still at Spanish Place we celebrated the centenary of St James's Church. The year was 1980. Cardinal Hume came to preach. The church had been cleaned inside and out, courtesy of Sir John Paul Getty (as I mentioned earlier), and the Sanctuary re-gilded. Before Cardinal Hume came to preach, I made a copy of a letter in the archives at Spanish Place. It had been written by Cardinal Manning (in his own hand) and was addressed to Monsignor Barry, then Rector of St James's. It was an apology from Cardinal Manning because ill-health had prevented him from coming to preach at the opening of the church. I sent the copy to Cardinal Hume in advance of his sermon at our centenary. He put it to good use too, as it provided the basis for his sermon on the day. One of the injunctions in Manning's letter (to Mgr Barry) was that he should address the people from the pulpit "but" added the Cardinal, "you need not preach for long". I don't know if Mgr Barry had a reputation for being long-winded; but clearly Cardinal Manning was taking no chances. Cardinal Hume took the point too!

Durrants Hotel is next door to the church and I always had a great relationship with Richard Miller, the owner, who was consistently kind to us. By way of celebration on our centenary, he invited me and my guests to have lunch at his hotel. When the church had opened in 1890 a lunch had similarly been held at Durrants for Mgr Barry and his guests. On that occasion the total bill had amounted to £9-18-01 (approximately (£9.90). The bill is still in the archives at St James's. In his extreme generosity, Richard said that the bill with which he would present me in 1990 would be a replica of the 1890 bill. £9.18.01 was something of a bargain for sixty people! The following day there was a cartoon in The Times depicting Cardinal Basil Hume offering a gratuity to the waiter in a lordly fashion, saying "Prithee, sir, accept this three-ha'pence for your trouble."

About this time it was my practice to go on holiday each year to Malta. I often went with Mgr Cormac Murphy-O'Connor, who was then Rector of the *Venerabile* in Rome, and later was – of course – to become Archbishop of Westminster. My younger sister, Pat, also accompanied us. We used to stay with the parents of boys I had taught at St Edmund's. They had retired there for tax reasons, and had a pleasant villa with a swimming pool in the garden. In those days I loved nothing more than an early morning swim. Cormac, lying in his bed shortly after dawn, used to say that he could hear "the patter of tiny feet" and a great splash as I took to the pool, after a running dive.

We also liked to swim in the sea at St George's Bay. It was about two hundred yards across the bay to the gardens of the rather smart Dragonara Hotel and Casino. One day Cormac and I decided to swim across the bay. We fetched up in the gardens of the hotel and got our breath back, sitting on the lawn in the sunshine. Suddenly from the hotel there came running past us Lord and Lady Monckton and their son, Jonathan – who knew Cormac as he was then the Bishop of their diocese of Arundel and Brighton. We felt slightly embarrassed as we were technically trespassing. Nevertheless, Cormac decided to brazen it out rather than hide, and greeted them airily!

Our holidays in Malta were great fun. Our hosts – the Ryans – always provided us with a car so we were able to see a lot of the island. These holidays continued until the Ryans died. As a priest, I am well aware of the kindness shown to members of the clergy by parishioners and friends. All my life I have felt as if I have been much blessed in this regard.

Another great blessing – which I have mentioned earlier – was to be invited regularly to cricket matches and generous hospitality at Sir Paul Getty's ground at Wormsley in Oxfordshire. On these occasions he always provided me with a chauffeur-driven car to fetch and carry me to and from the event. On one occasion I was sitting in the back of the car and the driver had a friend of his sitting in the front passenger seat. They chatted together in an easy manner about life in general. The passenger was recounting to the driver an occasion in the past when he had taken his wife to Paris for a weekend. "Of course," he said, "We wasn't married then", and over his shoulder (in the best cab driver fashion) added apologetically "... ooh, sorry Monsignor." The conversation continued along similar highly dubious lines, and liberally peppered with "Oh, Sorry Monsignor", as we sped along our route. When we eventually reached our destination I got out of the car, thanked them and said, "Now you can speak freely!" Ever since then, whenever friends of mine to whom I have related this delightful story – whenever they mention something slightly shocking, they always pop in a "Ooh – sorry Monsignor!"

CHAPTER XXIX

Hatched and Despatched

As Catholics I think we can be said to be fairly philosophical about death. The resurrection of the body being one of the essentials of our faith, we should be able to speak about death without inhibition. We believe that when someone dies their soul leaves the shell of their body behind, and while this deserves respectful treatment, there is no need for fear. As a priest, of course, I have attended many death beds and officiated at innumerable requiem Masses.

I remember once being telephoned by a Coroner. He told me that there was a body in his mortuary which required formal identification. He believed the body to be that of a man who lived in my parish, and wanted me to find somebody, living in the same block of flats, who might be able to identify his body. I realised that the most likely candidate for this was an occasional parishioner of mine. She was in her sixties and fairly melancholic. Just the person to take to a mortuary, I thought. She didn't let me down.

After a case of mistaken mortuaries, we finally arrived at the viewing chamber of the Westminster Coroner's Mortuary. The body was that of a poor unfortunate man who had jumped in front of a tube train. It was wheeled out for our inspection, and when my sad little lady expressed herself as uncertain of the identity, I asked if the body on the trolley could be presented from another angle. But this was not practicable. The little lady was still hesitant; she hummed and haa-ed a little, and finally said, "Have they got any others?"

I explained gently that the purpose of the exercise was to identify that particular body, not hunt around trying to find another. In any case, I didn't really want a procession of trolleys with corpses on them being wheeled before us. Eventually I had the bright idea of asking the attendant if we could see the clothes that the man had been wearing. He brought in a black plastic bag with various items of clothing. I asked the lady if she recognised any of these clothes. After a little persuasion she agreed that she did, and we were able to take our leave – with the body formally identified.

I do hope that this little tale has not offended your sensibilities. I think it goes to prove that – whatever the situation – humour is never too far away. I am, by nature, an extremely un-squeamish individual. I am the sort of person who will watch a heart and liver by-pass operation on television while tucking into my supper – oblivious of the gore. I have been told on many occasions that I could easily have been a surgeon, if a lack of squeamishness were the only requirement and if I had not had my priestly calling.

At the opposite end of the spectrum of life, we have birth. I am a great advocate of the school Nativity play. In these politically-correct times, there are fewer and fewer of them, but when I was a parish priest they were quite common.

I was a governor of the parish school, St Vincent's in Marylebone, for twenty years. In that time I saw many Nativity plays. I always admired the resourcefulness of the beleaguered school teachers who had to find a part for every child in the class. You could only have so many angels and shepherds without overloading their ranks! In an effort to cast a greater number of major roles, the more imaginative teachers treated the concept of the nativity with an admirable freedom, extending the scope beyond that of the usual story.

I can remember one teacher who decided to embrace the Visitation of Mary to her cousin Elizabeth as a prelude to the

Nativity proper. The Visitation scene consisted of a small performer knocking on an imaginary door, behind which there stood Elizabeth with broom. 'Our Lady' announced, "I'm going to have a baby." "So am I", said 'Elizabeth'. They hugged each other. End of scene.

There was a programme on the radio one Christmas-tide when listeners were invited to telephone in with their experiences of Nativity Plays. One lady reported how her son had come home declaring that he had been allocated the part of the clown. ?! It was then suggested that he could only have been – surely – the well-known 'Little Clown of Bethlehem'. Another child had been given the part of the pig in the stable. (A pig? In a Jewish stable?!) Yet another had been selected to be one of the dancer's with Salome of the seven veils fame. Quite where that fitted in with the Nativity story is obscure.

The renowned actress, Dame Judi Dench, tells the story of her daughter, Finty, at the age of about six or seven. She was given the role of the inn-keeper's wife – a part devised by yet another harassed and resourceful teacher. Judi recounts how she had some guests to dinner one evening. The guests dutifully enquired of Finty how she was getting on at school. "I'm in the Nativity Play," the little girl said proudly. "What part are you playing?" they asked interestedly. "I am the inn-keeper's wife." "And what is the play about?" she was asked. "It's about an inn-keeper's wife," came the immediate reply. This proved to be wonderful fodder for a Christmas sermon of mine on the temptation we all probably have of putting ourselves at the centre of everything. It was also a useful reminder of how we are all important in God's eyes – whatever part we have been given. In God's great orchestra, even the tin-whistle player has a vital contribution to make.

I recall one of the presenters of Radio 4's '*Today*' programme telling another delightful school Nativity story. Apparently one little chap had his nose put out of joint when his teacher overlooked him for the rather important part of Joseph, and cast him in the lesser role of the innkeeper. Joseph followed his lines carefully and asked if there was any room at the inn. The piqued innkeeper replied, "Yes – of course – come in, we have plenty of room!" Unfazed by this change in script, Joseph looked past the mischievous innkeeper into his inn, and said to his wife, "Come on, Mary. You wouldn't want to stay in a place like this." And with heads held high, Mary and Joseph made their exit in the direction of the prescribed stable.

The practice at Spanish Place was to erect an almost life-size crib in the garden. It was a beautiful crib and gave a very visible reminder to people of the real reason behind the great festival of Christmas. In one particular year it was an even greater success. My New Zealand curate, Fr Peter Keenan, a more than usually imaginative young man, conceived the idea of tethering a pair of small real ponies on either side of the crib. They were supplied with hay for their sustenance and were housed in 'stables' below the pavement in the evening. Everyone seemed very pleased with the result and they did their job of attracting a good deal of attention from passers-by in George Street. But you will always come across people who will find fault. This scheme provided one of them. When people expressed concern to Fr Keenan at having the ponies stand out by the crib for a few hours each day, he told them, "Look here! If they were down at their own farm in Hampshire they would be out in the meadow all day. They're much better off here sheltered from the wind." And if they objected that out in the country the ponies could run around and keep themselves warm, he would explain to them that horses don't run around to keep warm – "only human beings do that." When the complainant insisted, saying, "But they can't run about. They have to stand around, and their feet get cold." "Feet?" said Fr Keenan, "They don't have feet. They have hooves and you don't get horses suffering from cold hooves." Quite apart from all the attention they drew to the crib, there was the added bonus of fresh manure for the garden – all of which was carefully hoarded and added to the compost heap.

At St Peter's Residence, the Sisters organise a 'Living Crib' every Christmas. The Nativity story is read, carols are sung and local children provide the *dramatis personae*. They enter the stage in batches corresponding to the theme of the carol being sung. "While Shepherds Watched their Flocks" brings on a group of shepherds; enter the Magi to the sound of "We Three Kings" etc. – you get the idea, I am sure. Every year – from about September onwards – the Sisters speculate as to which of the local girls might be able to provide a baby in due season! It can get very nail-biting!

CHAPTER XXX

A Few Parishioners

It is not possible to be the rector of a central London parish – or indeed, any parish, without coming across a variety of characters. I have already mentioned the 'gentlemen of the road', but there were quite a few fairly eccentric personnel among the parishioners. There was a wonderful lady, Patricia Gibson, whom my predecessor referred to as 'Goldilocks' for reasons which should be obvious. Patricia was of a slightly melancholy turn of mind. On one occasion, before I had had my hip replacement surgery, I was talking to her at the church gate. She remarked "We are all *very* worried about you." I said, "There's nothing very much wrong with me. I just have to use this stick." "But what are you *doing* about it?" she asked. "I am going to see the surgeon on Thursday," I replied. "Will he amputate?" she said with a concerned look. I told her that I thought there were probably other options open to him!

There was also in the parish a wonderful woman called Nora Bradshaw. She was a real salt-of-the-earth character. For many years she organised the refreshments in the social centre, after the main Sunday Mass. Father Brian Darcy, a regular contributor to Radio 2's *Pause for Thought*, brought – on one of his visits to London – a shamrock plant, which he had dug up from Downpatrick, and 'smuggled' into mainland Britain. One day I was examining this plant and Nora was present. I explained carefully to Nora that it was a shamrock plant all the way from Northern Ireland. "Oh," she exclaimed," I thought shamrock had four leaves." Since the legend runs that St

Patrick explained the Blessed Trinity by reference to the three leaves of a shamrock, I remarked to Nora that I thought I should have a word with her about her theological knowledge surrounding the Trinity! She was somewhat flustered, but took the point well and joined in with the laughter.

Another of my ex-parishioners who leads – or claims to lead – a very quiet and secluded life, was receiving spiritual direction from the delightful Fr Donal Corry, whom I have mentioned earlier. At one point this woman said, "You see Father, I don't really have much opportunity to sin greatly." Dear Donal tried to disguise his laughter as he said, "What I think you mean is that you don't encounter many occasions of sin." When this little story was related to me later I commented that to describe it as "opportunity to sin" did suggest a certain enthusiasm for the subject!

There were so many wonderful people in that parish. In my time there was – and still is – Rosemary, who had been a parishioner for years before I went there, and who was always ready to engage in lively theological debate; there was Agatha, a delightful bouncy, enthusiastic Kenyan who nearly knocks me over every time she sees me with the vigour of her hugs; there is little Dora, who suffers much and yet is always grateful for the things she has; there was little Eileen and her late husband, Albert – you never saw a more devoted couple; there was Ardele who was always ready with a needle and thread to effect repairs; there was Bill, solid, trustworthy and thoroughly good; there was Betty – not a parishioner – but a regular visitor to the church. She was a remarkable sempstress of church vestments and an irrepressible character. She used to hold Patricia and Thelma spellbound in the office with her tales of the drama that was her life as a priest's housekeeper in Kennington Park; and there were so many more, too numerous to mention; all great characters and warm and kindly people who were good enough to take me to their heart and remember me in their prayers.

During one of my stays in hospital, I was visited by many parishioners – God bless them all. One or two of them could be a little on the doleful side, bringing me news of funerals and bereavements. With a smile, I confess at times to feeling a little like the prophet Job, being visited by his Comforters, who "sat for three days and three nights and said never a word, for the greatness of their grief." This was particularly true of dear Florence (God rest her) who suffered from severe deafness. I tried to make conversation, but she couldn't hear me. She tried occasionally to say something with her very quiet voice – and I couldn't hear her. So we sat in silence for half an hour or so and then she left.

Speaking of Job, I am reminded of the wonderful story from P G Wodehouse when one of Bertie Woooster's aunts is besieged on all sides by disasters. She eventually says to Bertie, "If the prophet Job were to walk in here right now, we could swap hard luck stories till dawn!" I am a huge fan of P G Wodehouse: one of my other favourite quotations from him describes a clumsy young man "who couldn't have walked across the great Gobi desert without knocking something over." Such a wonderfully picturesque description! Also, in these days when one reads of extraordinary names imposed upon newborn infants, I am reminded of Bertie's comment to his valet, "There's some raw work done at the font, Jeeves!" And ain't that the truth?!

CHAPTER XXXI

Preparing to Retire

After 15 years teaching, 12 years at Archbishop's House in Westminster and 22 years as Rector of St James's Church, Spanish Place, I had somehow managed to reach the age of 72. As you know, along the way, I had collected a new hip, a certain amount of arthritis, blood pressure a little higher than one might call ideal, had suffered a stroke which – thanks be to God – left me with little more than a weakness down my right side, and a slightly weak leg from the aneurysm surgery: really not too bad a tally for three score years and twelve. I was still going strong and enjoying my life as PP of one of central London's larger and busier churches. And I would have been happy to stay there until the Cardinal, or the Good Lord, decided it was time for me to go.

But then my eyesight started to cause me problems and I was diagnosed as suffering from macular degeneration, which as the name suggests, is a degenerative condition of the retina. Nothing could be done; I had to accept the fact that my eyesight would get gradually worse over the months and years. At first, the problem was not too severe. I could read in bright light with the aid of strong spectacles and, eventually, magnifying glasses of assorted strengths.

I should explain that one of the effects of MD is to remove from sight the beginnings and ends of words, so reading becomes something of a guessing game. In my office, at my desk, when I had plenty of time to screw up my eyes and peer, the affliction was less of a problem. At the lectern on the Sanctuary or in the pulpit, it was a different matter. After 49 years of reading the Gospels I was pretty familiar with them, and my congregation was always patient and understanding if I faltered. And then one day I read from the Gospel that Christ had angrily ordered the money-sellers and traders in the Temple to remove their 'pigs' from God's house of prayer. The word should, of course, have been 'pigeons', but the –eons had faded from sight and I was making a guess – as it turned out, not a very good guess! The likelihood of the Jews keeping pigs in their temple was fairly remote! Perhaps I only imagined that there were indulgent smiles from those whose attention had not wandered too far.

Nevertheless, it was around about then that I decided I should tender my resignation to Cardinal Hume and stand aside for a man with good eyes to take over.

In one of those instances of unfortunately bad timing, I was then offered some help in the shape of a willing parishioner who began to type out in large print what I needed for daily Mass. This meant that I could have carried on for several more years – but it was too late – my job had been filled. I was on my way to a Residence run by the Little Sisters of the Poor in south London. My retirement was about to begin.

Of course, before I could leave my spacious home at the Rectory, I had to clear my belongings and try to decide what had to be discarded and what could be kept, to fit into the small flat into which I was moving. I have to admit that, while I am reasonably tidy, the one area which had escaped any tidying for a number of years was my office – and particularly, my desk. The parish priest of any church gets a lot of mail, and I was (and still am) not good at throwing things out. I also have a habit of writing notes to myself on the back of used envelopes! Not a very efficient method of keeping track of things.

There was a mountainous pile of 'stuff' on my desk. Once again a helpful parishioner breezed in one day, determined that the desk was to be tidied. She picked up the pile, put it on her knees and went through every piece of paper with me, ruthlessly throwing away things which had gone way past their "do-something-about" date. Part way down the pile we came across my School Certificate. "By the time we get to the bottom of this pile I fully expect to find the Ten Commandments. On their original tablets of stone," she muttered. It wasn't *that* bad – but not far off.

When the desk had been cleared I was delighted to find that it was quite a smart leather-topped affair. I hadn't seen the surface of the desk for so long, I had quite forgotten!

I also had a vast number of books. My dear sister, Pat, applied herself diligently to the task of trying to sort out those I should take and those I should leave, or give away. What a job – I love books and would have been quite unable to face up to that job myself. Although my eyesight is poor, I usually have at least three books 'on the go' at any one time. And if I catch sight of a newspaper, the books are put aside immediately. It's the strong Irish in me.

On the day of the move, 23rd September 1998, we bundled ourselves and as much as we could manage, into a couple of vehicles and headed south to Vauxhall, SW8. Once we had arrived, Pat and a few helpful friends then set about stowing my bits and pieces away. They managed marvellously. I was installed.

CHAPTER XXXII

The Retirement Years

St Peter's Residence is a modern, well-run home caring for about eighty elderly people of mixed levels of incapacity of mind or body. Some are permanently confined to their rooms, others are able to lead fairly normal lives with their own rooms or flats, and all catering, cleaning and laundering provided. The nuns are a wonderful band of people, as are the carers and helpers, whose invariable cheerfulness belies the unattractiveness of some of the work they have to carry out.

As a fairly *compos mentis* priest, I was given my own little flat consisting of a bedroom, bathroom, sitting-room and – something of a novelty in my experience – a kitchenette. This last contained a fridge and a sink. It was not long before I was kitted out with a kettle, a toaster and a small, single ring, gas stove of the sort you might take camping. That was me set up for great culinary creations.

All my life I have been lucky enough to be cared for – mostly by nuns. I have never had to do laundry or housework or cook for myself. I was on a steep 'learning curve' – more a 1:1 learning incline. I have always loved cheese; most cheese, but especially cheddar cheese. And I am very fond of the lightly scrambled egg. My speciality was a combination of the two: eggs with a not inconsiderable amount of grated cheese whisked in and then cooked in a buttered frying pan. I'm mildly surprised that I couldn't hear my arteries screaming for mercy. My cholesterol levels were measured after I suffered a second very mild stroke a couple of years later, and the results bore testimony to the injudiciousness of my evenings over the camping stove with the eggs and cheese. I hadn't realised to what extent I had made this an almost daily supper, until a friend telephoned me one morning and asked what I was doing. "Grating cheese", was my reply. There then followed a discussion, heavy with irony, about the need for me to find and pursue really worthwhile hobbies and pastimes. I realised I would have to extend my culinary repertoire.

Not long after I started the self-catering in my kitchenette, I became intimately acquainted with the smoke alarm. I've always maintained that it is far too sensitive. The slightest puff of steam or smoke and off it goes. I know the idea is that the alarm should be shrill enough to wake everyone from the deepest sleep – but really. And it's not as if I can silence the wretched thing once it starts. The good nun who is Head of Smoke Alarms has to go to the master switch and turn it off after she has satisfied herself that there is no inferno, but just me cooking. It wasn't always me. But I'm ashamed to say that it often was. I do have an extractor fan, but the memory is taking sides with the eyes and the ears – it's fading in sympathy with them. I think the worst incident was when I came home quite late after being away for a few days. I decided at about 10pm that I was in need of toast. And, you've guessed it: within five minutes the corridor outside my flat was full of nuns in dressing gowns. On the plus side, at least they always knew where to start looking. On the odd occasion when it was not my doing, I would rush out into the corridor proclaiming my innocence to anyone who wasn't considering the possibility of evacuating the premises.

I love the characters you meet in any residential home – or any place where people are gathered together for some length of time; there is always such a mix, and in an elderly people's home, there is an even greater scope for eccentricity.

At St Peter's there are – as you might expect – more elderly ladies than men. The number of retired priests hovers around ten, and there are a few other senior gentlemen, but the majority of the gentlefolk are women. One of these ladies is over 100 years old and in full possession of her faculties, though not very mobile. I say that, yet she is mobile insofar as she tears about the place in an electric wheelchair, the driving of which she has mastered remarkably well. It is said that there have been no fatalities – but the jury is still out about one gentleman who received her full impact as she reversed out of a lift which he was waiting to enter. I'll say no more.

There is another dear Irish lady who vowed "if I pre-decease you, Monsignor, I'll bequeath my eyes to you." I had to explain gently that I didn't think eyes could be transplanted, but a whole head transplant was perhaps not altogether impossible!

And then there is Mary who has almost lost her sight and whose hearing is also deficient. She spends a good deal of time in the chapel at Mass tut-tutting and sucking in her breath in exasperation at any lacunae which may occur. She also mutters – more loudly that she probably realises – along the lines of "Oh, get on with it!" "What's he saying?" I can't hear him!" There was one memorable occasion when she was convinced that the priest at Benediction was inordinately slow. While he was at prayer before the Blessed Sacrament, she piped up helpfully the first line of the Divine Praises: "Blessed be God."

And there was cantankerous Kitty who, on one occasion when I paused to give her a blessing at the request of her carer, gave me a very strange look and said, "Is he serious?" Dear Kitty – God rest her – was much loved by her carers, despite her regular shows of impatience.

And then there are the wanderers. I used to leave the door to my flat permanently open, until I awoke one night to find someone standing beside my bed staring at me. It was a little unnerving, but I soon found a carer to re-unite this wanderer with her room. There was another wanderer who used to come in during the day and sit down in my little sitting-room, convinced that she belonged there. It's a confusing world – that which is inhabited by the elderly and slightly bewildered. There but for the grace of God go all of us.

There is also Streatham. I have been going to a care home, called St Mary's, three times a week for a number of years to celebrate Mass. This is the only chance of getting to Mass that most of the elderly folk there have. I have to admit that they are a fairly somnolent group at St Mary's; many of them are in a less robust condition than those at St Peter's. There is a resplendent front row of sleeping wheelchair users, one of whom is an enthusiastic concelebrant of mine: enough said! It is a smaller home than St Peter's, and the chapel, too is quite compact. The home is run by three delightful nuns of the order of Servants of the Mother of God. They are all Irish and, while the senior nun, Sister Rose Carmel is more serious and reserved, the other two (Sister Assumpta and Sister Martha) rejoice in a wonderful sense of humour.

Sister Assumpta especially is always on the look out for good Irish jokes – or even terrible Irish jokes. A favourite is the one about Murphy who tells Mick, "If you can guess how many ducks I have in dis sack, you can have de both of dem." Mick replies, "three". "Near enough," says Murphy, and gives him the ducks. Another favourite, concerns Mick and Pat who were passing a wood yard where there was a sign declaring "Tree Fellers wanted". "What a pity Seamus isn't with us; we could have gone for that job," says Mick. One more, the last I promise. Pat asks Mike, "Did you see Mulligan those days?" "Well," said Mike, "I did and I didn't." "What do you mean by that?" "Well, the other day, I thought I saw Mulligan and he thought he saw me. But when we got up close, we realised it was neither one of us." You have to say all of these jokes with a very heavy Irish accent to get their full benefit!

I could go on – but I won't. We swapped dozens and dozens of stories over the seven or so years that I said Mass at Streatham. However, for all I know there is a copyright on these jokes! And they are almost certainly terribly politically incorrect.

Some years ago the sacristan at St Mary's was a nun called St Anselm, God rest her. She was pretty elderly and a little hard of hearing. One day she took to me one side and asked me if I could keep my modest sermons on Sunday "down to five minutes." The reason she gave was that the "old ladies get fidgety" if I were to go on for longer. It was a lovely thought that that particular congregation could get fidgety at all, as there was barely a sign of a pulse among the lot of them! But of course it was no hardship to comply. So many of them were 'confused'. I celebrated Mass there for them one Ash Wednesday, and as I passed among them distributing ashes, many of them held out their hands or stuck out their tongues, believing I was bringing them holy communion.

On another occasion I celebrated Mass on Ash Wednesday at St Peter's Home. The good nuns there were determined that no one should miss out on receiving the ashes, so I was led around the home, crossing the foreheads of everyone who had been unable to get to holy Mass – including a couple of elderly ladies who were in the little hairdressing salon with their hair in curlers, and – after I had left – with a smudge of ash on their foreheads and a bewildered look on their faces. The same applied to several people who were sitting outside the doctor's surgery awaiting their turn to see the GP.

It is sad that, as I write, St Mary's Home in Streatham has been sold and Mass is no longer celebrated there – to the best of my knowledge.

So life goes on. When I reached the age of 80 I had a marvellous party at St Peter's. About a hundred people came to a very special Mass, which I concelebrated with some dear priest friends, including Andrew Wadsworth who delivered a marvellous homily and was there to offer that familiar strong arm to help me up and down the steps. There was some lovely sacred music – the wonderfully talented Elizabeth Nash sang a favourite of mine: Mozart's *Laudate Dominum*. And we kept the music going at the tea party afterwards when a String Quartet played some beautiful cheerful tunes as a background to the animated chatter. It was a lovely occasion and I was greatly humbled at the number of people who came to join in with the celebration.

My time at St Peter's passes peacefully (when I am not setting off the smoke alarm). I am visited regularly by ex-parishioners. I similarly receive many invitations to go out for meals with these good people.

I also visit Scotland for a couple of weeks each summer. I have a friend up there, a retired lieutenant-commander, named Rupert Craven, who lends me and my sister, Pat, a cottage near Thurso – which is about as far north as you can get without falling off the end. All in all, I now have no need, nor desire, to be miserable (cf. opening line of opus).

I have led a life full of happiness, blessings and many kindnesses. I can remember, for example, a number of occasions when taxi drivers have refused to take a fare from me, saying instead "That's all right, Farver – put it in the poor box." I mention this because it makes me think of a friend of mine who – on hearing that this happened – remarked, "Good old Monsignor; fallen on his little clerical feet again." And he was right: there have been so many, many occasions when I seem to have 'fallen on my little clerical feet' – and I am so grateful for that.

I have to say a huge thank you to all the many people who still remember me and – most importantly – continue to pray for me. I recall years ago, going to a retreat for priests where the opening salvo was, "Most priests go to hell." It's a sobering thought which has stuck in my mind; so I would be grateful – very grateful – if you would keep on praying for me from time to time, as I will for you. May God bless you.

LAUS   DEO   SEMPER